HE'S NOT PERFECT.
I'M NOT PERFECT.
BUT TOGETHER WE'RE...

PICTURE *Perfect*

SPECIAL EDITION

LAKIA BRANDENBURG

He's not perfect. I'm not perfect. But together we're…
Picture Perfect

www.lakiabrandenburg.com

Copyright © 2011, 2012 by Lakia Brandenburg
Special Edition © 2017

All rights reserved. No part of this book may be reproduced or transmitted in any form or by any means without written permission of the author.

ISBN: 978-0-9837182-1-5

Library of Congress Cataloging-in-Publication: 2017930979

Perfectly Imperfect Publishing Company, LLC

Printed in the United States of America

Live happily ever after ... for real! This book is dedicated to every woman who has ever been sold a fairy tale. After reading the pages of this book, I sincerely hope you will begin to believe in your ability to pen the pages of your very own picture perfect love story.

To Derek, my husband, thank you for penning the best pages of my life. Your love and support could never be measured. You have always believed in me, and for that I am forever grateful. I THANK GOD for giving me a real-life Prince Charming.

FOREWARD

Do you want to take your relationship to the next level? Are you hoping to break down barriers and climb mountains in your marriage? If so, Lakia Brandenburg has penned a powerful, must-read book for you. It provides balanced, practical instructions on how to create or recreate a fulfilling relationship with your spouse or your husband to-be.

Lakia takes readers on a journey from meeting a prospective mate to realizing that dream marriage. When I, Joseph B. Washington, a motivational speaker known nationwide, met Lakia, I knew I would buy her book. Her title alone sold me. *He's not perfect. I'm not perfect. But together we're...Picture Perfect* delivers a powerful punch.

After writing my book, *Let Average Go: 7 Keys to Turn Your Average into Awesome* and following years of mentoring people across the nation, I can sense a striking potential through people's presence alone. And Lakia's spirit personifies what her *Picture Perfect* roadmap spells out: creating your happily ever after.

Readers can shed all of the challenges of their relationships and follow Lakia's journey to a "Picture Perfect" marriage.

Joseph B. Washington
World Acclaimed Motivator and Speaker

CONTENTS

Foreword	7
The Perception of Marriage	11
A "Mr. Right" Fantasy	19
A Diamond in the Rough	23
Grand Duke of O.B.	33
The Encounter	41
Finding My Way	49
Always a Bridesmaid, Never a Bride	65
Do You Believe in Magic?	75
The Breakup	85
Before We Say, "I Do."	95
The Fairest in the Land	105
There's Power in the "P"	111
Creating a Happily Ever After	117
We Are One	121
What Did You Say?	125
It's a Heart Thing	131
No Love Jones	137
Money Tales	147
Day-to-Day Operations	161
It's Our Anniversary	165
Remember Why You Said, "I Do."	171
Meet LB	176

 THE Perception OF MARRIAGE

*"Marriage is a fine institution,
but I'm not ready for an institution."*

– Mae West

I recently read a report on ajc.com saying that marriages are becoming obsolete. I just knew there had to be something wrong with this article. How could anyone come to this conclusion about the highest sought-after position in the land? In other words, what woman didn't desire to live happily ever after with her prince charming? I thought every woman wanted to get married and that marriage was supposed to be blissful where I'm always in love and making lots of it. But where did I get that idea from? I was confused by what I read online and wanted some real answers.

Whenever I would ask newly married couples or couples who have been married for a few years about their views on marriage, each of them would give their own perception of what marriage meant based on what they've witnessed other married couples experience, fairytale stories, TV and movies, or maybe what they thought it was supposed to be. Not to mention many people were getting married (or not) for all sorts of reasons—mostly for wrong because their views of marriage were created by someone else. It was never based on what they intentionally created for themselves.

In some cases, women simply wanted to put down their "Me Phi Me" label and join the sisterhood of wives, while others were looking to fill a void or solicit bragging rights ("I's married now"). Singles would say that they were ready to settle down after living a fun-filled, adventurous single life. But to settle meant to accept whoever was available, despite what they had to offer—even if it required sacrificing your happiness.

So, basically, having a wedding ring on your finger was symbolic to wearing a small set of handcuffs. They were no longer "free" to enjoy life; they were now in legal bondage. Maybe this is one of the reasons why couples are choosing not to marry. Who would want to live this type of life? I began to think that the claims (including mine) were all based on perception. Could it be that the perception of marriage we've witnessed in our lives or even experienced has given us little hope of living the storybook fantasy?

I started thinking about the wedding and wondered if a bride and groom truly understands the step they are making (and the roles that come with it) when they decide to tie the knot. I honestly believe that too many women get caught up in the actual event of "getting married," making it all about becoming a bride just to gain the wife title by default. Apparently not long after the wedding festivities have ended, some couples are realizing that the expectations for this highly anticipated status are overrated. They spent more time and energy in becoming a bride only for a few hours rather than preparing to fully function as a wife. Maybe this is part of the reason why the perception of marriage is flawed and why marriages are becoming less popular. Now, don't misunderstand me. Your wedding day should indeed be special; however, spending countless hours of planning and tens of thousands of dollars on "one day" doesn't mean that your marriage will be successful. It's just an intro to your happily ever after story that you will soon share with your new husband.

Still somehow, for many couples, all of the love created on the wedding day couldn't sustain the test of the first year of marriage (which I've often heard was the hardest). And sadly for many others every year after that. Newlyweds may find themselves constantly "working on their marriage" or "trying to make their marriage work." They are working to save their marriage when actually they are supposed to be living the "perfect," love-struck life.

Let's talk about the word *work*. I've been told that marriage is work, and I guess that's expected. Anything worth having is worth working for, right? The question is, what kind of work will a couple endure just to keep the happiness alive? Truth is, I believe there's good work and bad work. But very few couples who I've been exposed to worked for the good, only the bad. They always unintentionally chose the latter.

Good work is where creation begins. Two whole individuals (filled with self-love and purpose) come together as one unit. The couple then gets educated about marriage and their roles, takes what they believe about this covenant and how it should be—within the parameters of God's definition, of course—and creates a relationship full of bliss, love, and everything that their

PICTURE *Perfect*

hearts desire. The good work confirms that marriage is what *you* create it to be, not what others *say* it's supposed to be.

Bad work means the couple possibly entered marriage with little or no preparation. One of my favorite quotes is "Jumping into marriage unprepared is as wise as jumping into a pool and not knowing how to swim." It clearly shows how not doing the right work can be devastating and in a lot of cases, deadly (divorce). The couple had no idea what they were signing up for and maybe their perception led them to believe that this wonderful institution of marriage was just supposed to work. (There's that word *work* again.)

But what about the marriages that appeared to be "working?" I was always looking at couples to see what made them work, or in most cases, not work. For many, the show—live and in color—was indeed a Broadway hit. The Joneses, the Browns, the Cunninghams, and the Smiths were living up to the storyline of their fabricated lives. They had the stunning home, the luxury vehicles, the successful careers, and the beautiful family—or at least it seemed. Behind closed blinds and shut doors, the couples were dealing with some real martial issues. If the reality of their story were told, it would read chapters of discontentment, unhappiness, and them often toying with the idea of ending their relationship in divorce. Bottom line, they weren't happy. They were pretending to be wrapped up in this fairytale marriage, when in fact it was a horror story.

As I observed the examples of marriages in my own life, I didn't understand why so many were either failing or unhappy. I came from the normal dysfunctional family where marriage was something that people just practiced. It was never set up to be successful or designed to last forever. It was never intended to be full of happiness. The reality of what marriage had become sure wasn't living up to my childhood dreams of what living happily ever after was supposed to be. I don't recall ever hearing the story about the happily devastating divorce, yet with a large percentage of marriages ending within the first eight years, it's society's everyday reality. Looks like divorce is burning up relationships faster than an arsonist with a license. Now that's scary! There truly is a thin line between love and lighter fluid.

I never thought that I would be happily married and have the marriage that would make others curious. They would see how their thoughts about marriage or even their personal experiences weren't aligned to the real-life example that stood before them. What made this couple different because this type of marriage was only considered a fantasy. Only actors in movies and fictional characters in the pages of a book experienced this type of happiness, right? But their perception was wrong. *This story* is a reality and I am the author.

Even though I tried, I couldn't blame my parents' failed marriage or the few examples of how a man and woman were supposed to live as husband and wife as my reasons for not making it through the "for better or for worse" times. I couldn't use that as an excuse to not be happy. I didn't need an *example* of what picture perfect looked like, because despite my upbringing, my personal experiences with love, and everything in between, I had to become the example that it does exist, not in a fantasy world, but in a reality that I created.

PICTURE *Perfect*

As you read my story about the journey of self-discovery, heartache, and the healing it took to have a *Picture Perfect* marriage, you will see that perfection has many descriptions. But I'm not talking about being flawless, excellent, or completely beyond improvement. It's about being able to take every detail of what imperfection is and shaping it into what perfection looks like to you. In every area of marriage, anyone can have an ideal picture perfect union. The power lies in you.

At the end of each chapter are reflection questions. Be honest and sincere as you respond to each question thoughtfully. Let this be the drafting stages of creating your own marital blueprint no matter if you're single, a soon-to-be bride, married, or divorced. Regardless of your past and how your perception was molded by others, you must understand that you have the power to create a *Picture Perfect* marriage (based on imperfections, of course) and have the ability to make it last forever. Marriage is a beautiful union that many people are choosing not to entertain because of their mindset and distorted ideas of this "institution." But perceptions can change. Your mindset can be renewed. We are all creators; therefore, you can create the marriage that you desire.

As you turn the pages of my story, keep this point of reference in your mind: Anyone who desires to have bliss, love, and happiness in your marriage no longer has to fantasize about it—you just simply have to create it to be your reality! Your story can be **Picture Perfect too.**

REFLECTION

1. What is your perception of marriage?

   _____
   _____
   _____
   _____
   _____

2. Which relationships and/or individuals played a part in shaping your perception of marriage?

   _____
   _____
   _____
   _____
   _____

3. Are you supposed to create the *Picture Perfect* marriage or is it just supposed to happen? Why or why not?

   _____
   _____
   _____
   _____
   _____
   _____

A "MR. RIGHT" *Fantasy*

As a little girl, I remember thinking that marriage was a fairy tale. It was a wish that remained dormant in my innermost thoughts and dreams. The next few years would be spent kissing frogs with hopes that one of them would transform into Mr. Right. But who could blame me. I didn't create this picture perfect image on my own. I was always seeing some handsome white prince charming, sweeping his unsuspecting princess off of her feet or hearing about the "love at first sight" stories where your chances of hitting Triple 7's on the Vegas slot machine were probably better.

We've all read about it. We've all seen it recreated on the big screen. So forget about this thought being made up, it had to be real! As the old cliché goes, things aren't always what they appear to be. One thing is for sure, I admired the picture perfect marriage based on a story with multiple authors. They say that a picture is worth a thousand words, but it's hard to believe that people would purposely depict the image in the wrong way. Someone must've experienced a marriage of perfection or this fantasized lifestyle.

PICTURE *Perfect*

But reality would paint a different image for me. Either countless examples of unhappy couples strangled my perception or individuals lied about how great married life was. It truly caused me to rethink my desire to blossom into the role of a wife. I would hear women playing the damsel in distress role seeking rescue from her real-life prince. They saw that their life would be transformed into royalty simply by being swept off of their feet. What really swept them was a tall tale.

Through the examples provided by my parents, family, friends, and in some cases coworkers or even actresses, I would come to understand one thing: I fell in love with the thought of getting married. I was overtaken by the thought of being a bride, or putting on a show. But time would later tell the truth.

For me, the portraits of marriage always reflected a relationship of pain, anguish, and regret—a direct contrast to what my expectations were. I couldn't understand why people shackled themselves before God and their guests pledging to live on death row for the rest of their lives. Where was the happiness painted in this picture? On the other end of the spectrum, couples portrayed a flawless relationship where everything appeared to be a picture of paradise. But it wasn't real.

As I replayed the nostalgic memories of my childhood, the illusion of the wedding day, and the love and happiness that was within a marriage, it all was based on what these couples created—period.

Over the years, I concluded that my favorite story was indeed a fable. Deep down inside, the women who shared the once-upon-a-time myth had good intentions. Their purpose was to instill some reason to believe that dreams do come true—even in relationships. But reality would later prove that prince charming was make-believe. His existence was merely an imagination: an image that fades to black as the truth behind the "happily ever after" tale revealed itself one wart at a time. There was no perfect marriage. Or was there?

In knowing this, and in thinking back to the relationships and marriages presented before me, I have to face one significant question: Will I let my little princess enter a fantasy world as I read her favorite fairy tale at bedtime? Perhaps my storybook romance is the one that will reflect the real meaning of marriage and true love or the ongoing fascination of a tale that may never come true.

The real story begins …

 A Diamond
IN THE ROUGH

> *"A diamond is a chunk of coal that is made good under pressure."*
>
> – Henry Kissenger

At one point in my childhood, I considered myself to be daddy's little princess. But as I developed into a young adult, that thought was my imagination and I certainly didn't inherit a dowry.

My childhood revealed different perspectives of marriage from every area of confusion to pain. I grew up in a suburban Maryland neighborhood lined with duplexes. There were four different relationships that I maintained under the roof of a three-bedroom, two-story home. Each relationship expressed a different kind of love. Being the youngest child, I witnessed love through various age levels and mediums—my two older siblings (one brother, one sister) and my two parents. Sometimes, the love was gentle, but mostly it was rough, selfish, and mean.

My parents' union was my first example of what married life was all about. I learned early on that my father wasn't a very affectionate man. Rarely did he hug me or tell me that I was beautiful. I can't remember ever talking to my father about boys, love, or relationships. I

PICTURE *Perfect*

actually think my father wanted me to be a boy. He treated me like his youngest son. Instead of "dating" me and teaching me what to expect from a man, my father was teaching me how to change oil and tires. He was more concerned with me being able to distinguish between a Phillips or a flathead screwdriver than explain how to be independent and play the dating game. I guess it just wasn't designed that way for my family.

His job was to be the provider and my father had a good government job. He worked nearly twenty years with the Postal Service. He was a serious man and always about his business. His form of affection was hard to read by outsiders. He evoked independence in his children by letting us do things my mother would object to. My mother, on the other hand, was a very caring woman. She valued, above all things, her family and education. She was protective of her girls and a true fan of all of our accomplishments. Her role was to nurture and play the warden of the house. The relationship that she and my father shared was typical of a middle-class working family. But love after several years of marriage painted a picture of turmoil and pain.

My parents were married for twenty years before they divorced. When I think about their relationship, spurts of bittersweet memories enter my mind. My mother used to always share stories of how my father was at one point in time a "good" man. I remember when they used to host card parties at the house. The backyard would be filled with friends and family who enjoyed celebrating a sunny day and warm weather with a cookout. These were the good times or good ol' days.

Their favorite outing together wasn't the typical

dinner and a movie. Their idea of a good time was in hand-dancing. I remember them getting dressed up to go out dancing often.

My mother would wear a dress and put on her make-up in the half-bathroom on the main level. I would sit on the top of the toilet in our small confined space to watch her transform into this beautiful dancer. I remember her hair being styled in a Jheri curl afro. She would pin one side up and place a flower in her hair. She looked like a señorita. She was gorgeous.

My father would dress in their bedroom upstairs. He was sharp in his button-down, long-sleeve shirt. He would always have his collar flipped up and his tie draped around his neck. He would leave the task of tying his tie to my mother.

When they stepped out of the house, they looked so happy. The bop and a fancy two-step was their favorite dance move. But soon the graceful dancing at local clubs turned into violent twirls around the stairs and rooms within the house. My father's charismatic charm would soon vanish.

I'll never forget the night that my understanding of marriage and love took a turn for the worse. After being awakened by the moaning sounds from my mother, I jumped out of my bed and ran downstairs to the living room. I could hear her crying from the vents in my room. The vents allowed you to hear sound bites from the basement. They would carry sounds of trash-talking and laughter from when my parents' friends were over to hang out and watch the game. But tonight, something was wrong. I didn't see it but could hear the sounds of punches being thrown, forming a mental note of the impact from my father's powerful blows landing on my mother's face. Right then, love became a sound of a battered woman pleading for her life. With every hit, my mother cried for mercy. I quickly picked up the phone and made a frantic 911 phone call. By this time, my mother had gathered up enough strength and crawled up the basement stairs to the same bathroom that she had used to transform into a classy dancer. The toilet that I had sat on was now filled with globs of blood that was pouring out of her face. She was unrecognizable. My father—for no cause—had beaten her like she was a stranger on the street.

As she looked in the mirror, she noticed her beautiful eyes that she would outline with eyeliner and mascara were now painted the color of black and blue. The red lipstick that I would watch her trace on her lined lips was now dripping blood. Her lips were no longer full from the application of a pencil liner but were swollen and split open like an overcooked hotdog. I couldn't believe what I was seeing. I felt like I was moving in slow motion. And so was the time. It felt like time had come and gone before help arrived.

Then time was interrupted by several hard knocks on our front door. It brought the present back into perspective. Standing on the other side of the door were two uniformed officers. There was no need to ask the routine "What seems to be the problem?" question. With just one look at my mother's face, they entered our living room and immediately cuffed my father for domestic violence. I remember my father kneeling on the carpeted floor in his bathrobe. He looked at me with a piercing stare as I walked past him, fearing repercussions of my actions. I never knew love like this before, and I never wanted to experience this type of love again in my life.

On this very night, my father renounced his thrown as royalty and head of our household. I replayed this night over and over, again and again, as the years went by. It took some time to trust a man the way my mother, at one time, had trusted my father.

My personal experience playing with love really didn't begin until I enrolled in college. Leaving behind my friends, I tightly held on to my scarred memories of what relationships looked like. In an attempt to change the way I viewed men, I began to open up and date. I knew that abusiveness wasn't an attribute that I was looking for in a man. Nor did I want to find a younger version of my father. But ironically, I discovered that the men, although not physically abusive, abused my desire of wanting to feel loved.

In high school, I was just an average student. I went to class, had my best friends to hang around, and simply admired the "cuties" in the hall. I didn't have a boyfriend. I only found myself daydreaming about sharing something special with the opposite sex. I was always wondering what it would be like to get with the popular light-skinned, pretty boy.

I really didn't start being "eye candy" until I entered my first year of college. I guess they don't call it fresh fish for nothing. I became an automatic target for mostly upperclassman. The attention I was getting from the New Yorkers, Georgians, Floridians, South Carolinians, and even my District of Columbians was quite flattering. Remember, I didn't even have a boyfriend in high school. How was it that I developed overnight into this attractive chic from Murland (how we said Maryland), who was known for wearing designer stretch jeans, a brand-named fitted top, or some slouched socks with Chuck Taylors?

Before getting a taste of the southern hospitality, my experiences with relationships were slim to none. I guess I could include the boy with the Gumby fade, who I called my boyfriend in the first grade. But as a young adult, I didn't learn anything other than the anatomy of a man. I was clearly naïve at every "ay girl," "pssst" that caught my attention. Attending class, partying with my girls, and being fooled by my admirers on campus was how I spent my early years in undergrad.

For three and a half of my college years, I was never anyone's girlfriend. I had my fair share of dates and practicing mission impossible stunts to sneak into the athletic dorms on campus. What can I say, at this stage in my life, I had a thing for athletes. I think I was subconsciously en route to be a basketball girlfriend-turned-wife. I remember going to all of the basketball and football games on campus, perpetrating. Sitting in the bleachers, I fantasized about having a celebrity boyfriend to call my own. Whenever they had games that were televised, I would pretend that I was supporting my man from home. (There I go daydreaming again).

When I finally took someone seriously, I experienced the most heartache ever. I was reeled in by an upperclassman and couldn't resist his bait. I remember this one Georgian causing the most devastating pain imaginable. He was a popular light-skinned, pretty boy who showed me "genuine" interest and even went through many hoops to get my number to eventually land the first date. (I guess I got my high school wish.)

He taught me that men are untrustworthy and that they will say anything to get what they want. I remember our first night out. He being a senior and I a sophomore, he picked me up from my dorm and took me to his rented house off-campus. When we arrived, arranged on the dinner table was my favorite meal: spaghetti and salad. He showed me through his actions that he had listened to me during the many hours of conversation that we shared. I was in love. A man cooking for me? I was in heaven. But I was so naïve. Even though all of the signs were there, I was too blind and too desperate to feel loved by a man. And the story would end: This same guy was a father of a newborn; his girlfriend was away from school on maternity leave. I was a space-filler until she returned after recovering from giving birth to his and her child.

But it didn't stop there. This pattern of being misled, used, and abused continued each semester as I tried my hand at finding love in a real relationship.

PICTURE *Perfect*

REFLECTION

1. Describe your childhood example(s) of love and marriage.

   _____
   _____
   _____
   _____
   _____
   _____

2. While growing up, what was your relationship with your father or any other male figure if your father wasn't around?

   _____
   _____
   _____
   _____
   _____
   _____

3. Describe your first experiences with love. What did you learn about men?

   _____
   _____
   _____
   _____
   _____
   _____

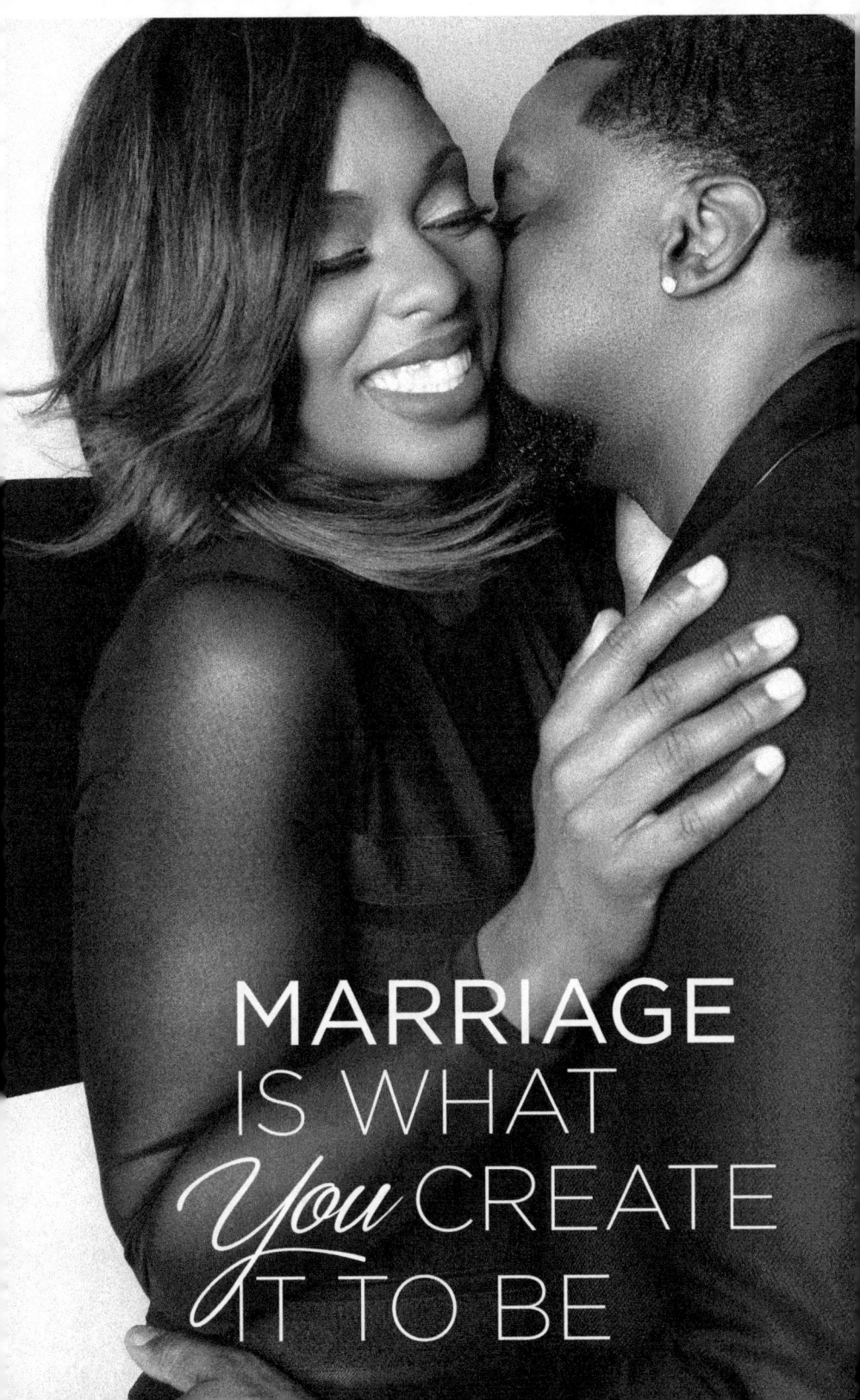

GRAND DUKE OF O.B.

"I'd kiss a frog even if there was no promise of a Prince Charming popping out of it. I love frogs."

– Cameron Diaz

S imply put, sex, drugs, and violence (SDV) raised Derek. His royal upbringing involved an immense consumption of this dangerous combination. His hangover would have lasting effects on the decisions he would ultimately make in his life—especially in relationships. A country boy from the backwoods of Orangeburg (O.B.), South Carolina, Derek thought he had everything figured out. There was just something about being from the South. Down in the dirty, things were done much differently. They claimed members of the neighborhood as their family. They were extremely close. No matter if you were blood or not, you were considered kin in some way.

The grounds of his well-known nook were built around a circle of single-wide trailers, dirt roads, and folk who loved to put food on the grill to spark up an impromptu barbecue. The bond between family and friends was priceless. To this day, this is something he loves about the place he will forever call home. It was nothing to cruise through the neighborhood, seeing the

PICTURE *Perfect*

residents or visitors who frequented "The Fair Grounds" posted up on the hood of their early-'90s model Cadillac Deville. Anybody of status would rock a wife-beater and some Dickies pants. When they spoke a dialect of southern Geechee drawl, you'd catch a glimpse of their gold fronts.

The community prided itself on the reputation that the area would formally be known as The Fair Grounds. It was like a county within itself. The residents took it upon themselves to make this place called home special. They started their own traditions. Each Thanksgiving, the older teens and adults would play a competitive game of semi-organized tackle football. Everybody showed off their athletic abilities during what can be considered their very own Super Bowl. It was a highly anticipated game of pad-free football. Players would suit up in the finest equipment. They would wear sleeveless hoodies over layers of t-shirts. To protect their neck and support the impact of being hit, the hood would be tucked in the back. Some of the players were members of the local high school football team. They would "borrow" jerseys from the school to make it official on game day.

Independence Day was reserved for fallen soldiers. Pictures of homies who were all killed, mostly due to violence, were ironed on the front of their t-shirts. It was a celebration of their souls being freed from their life on The Fair Grounds. Their names would forever be uplifted and never forgotten. In a nearby grassy area, you would find the talents of all local NBA hopefuls, shooting basketball on their homemade basketball court. The basket was a bucket that was nailed to a metal pole. The neighborhood grandma ran her own local store out of the living room of her double-wide trailer. Regular customers could buy snacks, such as candy and chips from the porch-sitting senior. She had everything. You could even buy a bag of weed from her.

Off the main road in the corner was the neighborhood juke joint. It was common to find patrons hanging outside sipping beer or a glass of moonshine. On the inside of the boarded club, partygoers would be shooting pool, betting at each call, "eight ball, side pocket." The soothing sounds of Sam Cooke, Johnny Taylor, and Bootsie Collins were blasting from the one speaker of the antique juke box. You would've thought that the owner hosted local karaoke when everybody sang along to Lenny Williams' *Girl, you know I-I-I-I-I love you*. This classic stayed on repeat.

Venturing outside the perimeters of the grounds wasn't necessary. Any and everything your heart desired was within arm's reach. Derek loved being on the block. Being raised by all women in a three-bedroom, single-wide trailer, Derek's models of manhood were slim to nonexistent. Although his uncles were around, they were too busy trying to survive. Thus, he relied on the streets to teach him how to be a man. Everybody on the grounds had one thing in common: They consumed a heavy sample of the SDV potion. Everybody around him either used or sold drugs, including members of his family. The role models were older cats who lived and died by the lifestyle. He admired the way they conducted business and picked up on their habits and ways of living. They taught him how to hustle and showed him what a man, according to the standard written by The

PICTURE *Perfect*

Fair Grounds, looked like.

By age 15, Derek had accepted his calling. He was a typical kid in the neighborhood always in some form of trouble. From season-to-season, there were games that he would participate in, making The Fair Grounds even better than a trip to Disney World. In the summer, he and his friends would break into the local golf course and steal golf carts. Racing and crashing down the course—all while being chased by the owners' four vicious pit bulls—was his example of amusement. Snow was a rarity in South Carolina. It was very seldom that a winter wonderland would descend on this end of the East Coast, but when it did, you'd best believe that the boys from The Fair Grounds took advantage of it. They found every way to corrupt childhood innocence. When most kids would make snow angels or build a snowman, fun snow ball fights would turn into brutal attacks. Each snowball would actually be used to cover a rock that was hidden in the center.

When it came to his inheritance, he credits his sales from drugs. Drugs were always available. Derek received respect from the neighborhood because of his connections to a well-known drug dealer. This helped parlay him into an entrepreneur enterprise. Drugs were never something that had to be looked for. It was available to use or sell any time or place. As Derek became more involved in the streets, the demand for drugs on The Fair Grounds tripled. As his customer base increased, so did his supply and profits.

Everyone was on something: weed, cocaine, crack, or liquor. A lot of the domestic abuse came into play because of these four drugs. This would later serve as

Derek's way with women. If women weren't the victim of being slapped around, they were victims of infidelity. The women in many cases weren't bothered by the cheating as long as they were getting status or financial support.

Sex was abused. There was an abomination of incest occurring too. Third and fourth cousins knowingly slept with each other. (I told you they were a tight-knit community.) Men were more loyal in their friendships with each other, rather than to a woman. Women were seen as objects. When it came to the agreements made with females, it involved cheating and more cheating. Girls were like drugs, they were always available on the block. When it came to girlfriends, having multiple women was a part of their culture.

Women played different roles in the lives of the men. For instance, women were used to playing a role of being an organizer, the other a transporter, or the undercover drug dealer. The drugs and women all circulated within the neighborhood. This became a competitive routine of the boys on The Fair Grounds. They even established an unwritten rule about sex with the women in their neighborhood.

The men controlled the women. Women were not allowed to have sex with any men outside the courtyard without sexing one of the royal members from The Fair Grounds first. If this happened, it would resort to violence. You would think that violence would've subsided with the police department being literally within walking distance, but it didn't. Violence came into play if any form of disrespect was involved. The same problems were revolving around every member of the neighborhood. There were a lot of neighborhood rivalries, and countless cases of men physically abusing their female companion. Nothing Derek did felt wrong because it was a community effort. It was the norm. It felt right. It was an endless circle that had been passed down from generation to generation.

After years of sowing his royal oats, Derek decided to retire, somewhat. By the time he experienced the karma of life and aged by years, not necessarily wisdom, his expectations of a relationship was soiled. The women that he was recruiting began making unusual requests. They actually wanted him to act like a gentleman. Derek was used to being in control, but found that he was challenged by these requests. He was a gallant. The women in his royal court wanted a charismatic knight, one who opened doors and showered them with gifts. Derek wasn't having it. He maintained his self-proclaimed womanizer title and continued to play the field.

He was used to a certain caliber of females and lifestyle, until he ventured outside of his comfort zone. He knew within his spirit that there was something different than what he was accustomed to doing. He never thought of marriage because of the models that were presented to him. A "happy" marriage was unheard of. There were a slim number of married couples Derek knew. During the day they would be "happy," but it was the Fourth of July when the lights went out and I don't mean a celebration with fireworks. Everyone knew what was going on behind closed doors, but it was an accepted way of life. Overall there wasn't anything happy going on and no reason to seek this type of commitment. Derek would remain truthful and married to the life that he devoted his time to on The Fair Grounds. But the desire for genuine deep love was a secret goal of Derek's. He just knew that there was something else to this thing called love. He wanted something different.

After some years, the cycle of life that he had grown accustomed to was getting old. The move from juggling multiple women to being able to be with one woman didn't arrive until someone different struck his interest. It took a woman, who came from a different type of upbringing, to offer a new intoxicating drink to the playboy.

PICTURE *Perfect*

REFLECTION

1. Describe your prospective grand duke's or prince's upbringing.

2. Describe his perception of marriage before you met him. How does this affect your future as a couple?

3. What is your grand duke's relationship with women?

The Encounter

"What counts in making a happy marriage is not so much how compatible you are, but how you deal with incompatibility."

– Leo Tolstoy

For years I wondered why I was attracted to the bad boy type. If your status was hood, it was all good with me. It was just something about a man with a hard exterior—you know, thug-like. It was a sign of protection. He could not only defend himself, but me too. He would be a man with a backbone who could carry his own. He would have so much swag that every female wanted him. Not to mention, he would come with fringe benefits. Being his girlfriend would bring about more identity. A lot of which was probably caused from me not knowing who I was. He would also have street credibility. Everybody would know him. To tell you the truth, I really didn't know what I wanted in a man … but I got exactly what I asked for.

Even before I understood it, I created my situation. I spoke Derek into existence. I was so specific about the outer appearance that I forgot about what really mattered. Not once did I mention how important it was that he treated me well. Nor did I define the purpose he would serve in my life.

I met Derek not expecting anything. Now I realize

that having no expectations was a mistake. I didn't give him purpose in my life from the beginning. I was a rising junior in college. My concerns were focused on having a good time with my friends and finishing school without becoming a super senior. If anything Derek would serve as a temporary spot like all of the other men in my past. Some people always say when you meet Mr. Right, you will know. Well, I didn't know anything about Derek or the future of our relationship. Remember, when it came to marriage it was a dream. It felt better to fantasize on that lifestyle than to expect it to come true. But there should always be standards—no matter what you do or who you meet. This goes back to creating your situation. If you don't set expectations, the story will pan out to be whatever life wants it to be. You are no longer in control, and you will be a victim of letting "nature take its course," like the old saying goes.

I remember it like it was yesterday. I was just a walk-in customer in need of a shape up. I was wearing the mid-'90s short cut of the R&B singer Monica and was referred to this barber by my other short-haired friend. As I sat in the black barber chair, a 10-minute fade quickly turned into a half-hour encounter. I knew that the back of my neck wasn't that nappy, but it was taking him a while to simply line me up. The conversation was so long and drawn out that, after a while, I couldn't figure out what we were talking about. I figured he was another dude just trying to talk to me on an I'm-trying-to-get-to-know-you level. I know I didn't have a reason for meeting Derek, but surely he had a reason for meeting me.

Several weeks prior to me coming into the barber

shop, Derek was at a local club partying with some of his friends. He was scoping out the scene when he noticed on the other side of the crowd, her. She was a slender girl in all black. The neon light from the bar shined through her mesh Iceberg designer top that flashed her black Victoria Secret bra. From the looks of her skintight pants, he didn't know where they began or ended. She was fine. He liked what he was seeing. For whatever reason, he didn't seize the opportunity to confront this work of art. The night ended, and the partygoers left the scene. She would later be known as the mystery girl.

Derek thought that she attended his school, just 30 minutes away from the main college campus. He knew that he would see her again somehow, someway. He was a local, so he knew everybody. Wherever she lingered, she would stand out like a tourist. But his efforts failed miserably as the woman in black was nowhere to be found.

He actually searched for her. There was something about her. He knew the physical attraction was there, but it was more. He didn't know what that more was, but time would tell as the story unfolds. Until that one day when she walked through the door of the shop. There she was—me.

I was what he was looking for. His expectations were already set. He knew what his plans were for me, on the other hand, I was the amateur. I didn't know the rules. The exchange of money for the service—not to mention a generous tip—would be the first move I made on the blackboard. I was young and didn't know that this one move would determine the next. Somehow money wasn't the only exchange that took place on this late

PICTURE *Perfect*

afternoon. He managed to slip his business card in my hand as we parted ways. This one day would mark the beginning of something that I had always failed miserably at. *Let the games begin ...*

Derek and I were like most couples who didn't know anything about the dating game. We dated off and on for years—eight to be exact. I remember our first date. Derek picked me up from my dorm in an old-school white Cadillac Deville. Everybody in this town must've owned this car. They came in every color too. This just so happened to be his first car. At the age of 21, Derek had finally purchased his own transportation. He took me to pick up his tags from an old rundown repair shop before we ventured out to Applebee's for lunch. The country-boy style was totally different from what I was accustomed to. I was used to my men from the DMV metropolitan area, wearing the signature slouch socks with Chuck Taylors. They had a southern Murland slang or Chocolate City flavor where every other word they said was "bama" and "young." But this would soon change.

There he stood in an overall jean jumpsuit with a pair of tan Timberland construction boots. It wasn't the most stylish ensemble I had seen, but it was a fixable situation. Already I was seeing if I could mold this man into what I wanted. If I would consider him a prospective mate, he had to work on his fashion. (This is bad work.) The next few weeks of seeing each other would quickly turn into months.

I met Derek in January and by June he started introducing me to family and friends, a protocol for a guy who was getting feelings for any female. I had passed all security measures after being screened for months. His results were in: I was harmless. I guess you could say after that, his trust for me began to grow. I was even invited to The White House. This place was monumental. The White House was the place that Derek called home. His "auntie" and best friend, along with another childhood friend lived there. His auntie was cool. She was the female influence in Derek's life. She was the type of auntie who played his surrogate mother. She taught him how to handle a woman from the perspective of a hood chic. She would club with Derek, smoke with Derek, even taught him how to play the field.

Now, we were in the South, so you know that his auntie could cook her behind off. She was known for her buttermilk, fluffy Jiffy cornbread, four-cheese macaroni, and perfectly seasoned fried chicken. I was definitely in there. But I would later find out that I wasn't the only female who often passed through the metal detectors. All of the residents of the house protected each other, especially Derek. I was supposed to be just another visitor passing by but unexpectedly became more.

We began to do more and more for each other as time progressed. Our feelings for each other were growing stronger, and we began to show each other another level of appreciation. I remember when I surprised Derek for his birthday with one of the best Jacuzzi suites that O.B. could offer. It was decked out with flowers, music, and candles.

Our relationship extended past the months when school was out for the summer. I had returned to Maryland as a part of my routine college schedule. My birthday was just two weeks away. Derek, never traveling

PICTURE *Perfect*

past South Carolina before, ventured up North and surprised me. I remember the excitement I felt when he walked through the kitchen door of my aunt's house. I ran upstairs out of confusion and surprise. I started crying. Our love was really real. I was liking Derek and his driving 10 hours just to spend my birthday with me was something special.

But it wasn't always birthday celebrations and tears of joy. I had my fair share of competing for the love of Derek on more than one occasion. First there was the confrontation at my part-time job. His ex-girlfriend approached me. Standing at barely 5'5, she challenged my ability to conduct myself as a lady. In a standoff debate, I—in a polo uniform top and khaki pants, and she in her hood-vixen best—had to pretend that I didn't believe all of the dirt she was revealing about my man who wasn't man enough for her. Sadly, I knew it was true. But I maintained my composure in front of her. You never let your enemies see you sweat, right? I walked away as a winner. I was still in the running toward remaining the new leading lady in Derek's life.

I performed quite well in the how-fast-can-you-back-your-car-out-of-your-boyfriend's-ex-girlfriend's-driveway-without-hitting-oncoming-traffic challenge. The scenario: Your reaction after seeing your man's car parked in his ex-girlfriend's driveway. That dangerous stunt placed our relationship on trial and really challenged our reasoning for being together.

If only we knew the rules of this game and what to expect beforehand. I've been told that it's good to date someone for at least four seasons. The wisdom behind this theory is that as seasons change, people do too. I needed to see who Derek was becoming in the winter, spring, summer, and fall. But there was too much time wasted between us. For Derek and I, the rules of dating were hard to follow. We simply played the game by making up the rules along the way.

At some point, Derek and I should've made a conscious decision about where our relationship was going. By not knowing how to play by the rules, we both lost out. We didn't know that if you landed on the wrong space on the board, you couldn't pass go. We missed out on a very important part of what some would consider the marathon to the altar. None of our married experts ever mentioned taking our relationship to the next level of courting. I told you, I didn't know how to play the game. We never discussed marriage, and I would later discover his true feelings about our future as Mr. and Mrs.

PICTURE *Perfect*

REFLECTION

---

1. How do you approach dating? If dating is a game to you, how do you play it?

   _____
   _____
   _____
   _____
   _____
   _____

2. How long do you think you need to date before knowing if there is chemistry or not?

   _____
   _____
   _____
   _____
   _____
   _____

3. What rules will you create for yourself as you play the dating game?

   _____
   _____
   _____
   _____
   _____
   _____

FINDING *My Way*

"Many are the plans in a person's heart, but it is the Lord's purpose that prevails."

– Proverbs 19:21

After graduating from college, I packed up my mid '90s Nissan Altima and relocated to Georgia. Derek moved in six months later once he completed the program for his degree. I had no job, only a strong ounce of faith to be something greater than what I was. I knew that I wanted to work in entertainment, but hadn't created a real plan to make it happen. For now, I was simply following the model that was presented for me: go to school, graduate, get a job, and move in with your man. Check. I was somewhat on schedule. I had everything but the job. My move to the South, I thought, was to find myself. I was badly seeking my niche in the corporate world.

When I finished my undergraduate degree, I was under the impression that I would have the best job. My mother was a strong advocate for graduating, emphasizing that it could help me land a "good" job.

I believe it was more of her dream than mine, since

PICTURE *Perfect*

she barely finished her freshman year at Howard University. Maybe I was living out her dream of attending an HBCU (historically black college or university) and walking across the stage with honors. That was the slogan my mother used to explain why I needed to be in college and not pursuing my dreams of modeling.

Modeling was so creative, so fun, so me. My sleek physique at the time, in addition to people always suggesting, "you should model," gave me hope that this might be something to look into. This was my Plan A. Every model call, casting call, calendar shoot—I was there. I even tried out for a cycle or three of the popular America's Next Top Model and was a semi-finalist to meet Tyra Banks on the then hit TV show, *Fanatic*. I could see myself strutting down the catwalk in major fashion districts such as Paris, Milan, and of course, New York City. I would spend hours practicing edgy poses and facial expressions in the mirror. If only I understood back then the strength in following your dreams. There was something there, but it was being downplayed. My perception was being clouded by individuals who were unable to follow their dreams. In turn, they told me that I wouldn't be able to do the same. To them, modeling was a dream. It was a hobby that wouldn't generate any money to pay bills. For the two-time presidential scholar and cum laude honor roll student, a good job was in selling clothes. Retail became my reality.

I guess you can say I was a store model. But this wasn't the type of modeling I was talking about. I felt cheated. I guess I should've asked more questions. My mother convinced me through savvy sales tactics, and now I was stuck searching for answers. I spent four years of living the American dream, or so I thought, to only get a degree and land a job that paid minimum wage. Am I being punk'd? I was waiting for a camera crew to rush me as I stood puzzled in disbelief.

My move to the Peach State was to find the sweeter things in life. There was just no way that working Monday through Sunday, opening and closing a high-end clothing store, was going to reflect my level of success in life, but it did. I spent long hours pacing the floor, folding and refolding clothes and greeting customers. I had to come up with a clever catch phrase to win over my clients just to get them to purchase an outfit. It didn't matter if it flattered them or not, that wasn't my concern. I had a sale to make to see a small percent increase on my paycheck.

I had crashed in a place of discontentment. I was miserable. I was in a state of mediocrity and was desperate for more. I had to take flight. If I was going to be landing anywhere, it was going to be a place that I felt reflected what I represented. Either I was coming to Atlanta to be a part of the fast-growing entertainment industry or to eventually go back to school to get an advanced degree. My options were slim, but it was a start. Besides, being a lifelong student had to be better than repeating:

"Can I help you find something today?"

Little did I know there was another big sale for me to make. I had my own agenda for my move, but would later discover that God sent me to Georgia to make the most commission that I could ever imagine in my life. He had plans for me. They were plans that would not only change my perspective on life, but recreate the love life that I always dreamed about.

PICTURE *Perfect*

The next couple of months would be a time of self-discovery, trials, and desperation. Derek was out-of-sight, out-of-mind—which created a lot of "me" time. Since the move to Georgia was mutual, we agreed to share the responsibilities of paying rent and utilities. He was trying to establish himself as a new barber and did his best to send money to help take care of our apartment. But ends were getting more and more difficult to meet. Remember, I was a college graduate holding on to the promises that my mother told me would happen just for completing this accomplishment.

The move to Georgia was definitely a leap of faith. I didn't have a job and convinced myself that I could get a job anywhere. My move was similar to someone chasing their dreams. But I was an artist who didn't know my talent. I did know the stories of successful individuals who had hit rock bottom before enjoying the good things in life. At this point, anything was better than working at a job that only required you to have personality and a love of fashion. I sure didn't need to go to college for that. I guess all of those stories about starving artists somehow encouraged me. But this starving artist was starving—literally.

I made several attempts to make my life into something I was proud of, but came to grips that my plan wasn't working. The bright lights in the entertainment field were dim, and all of the letters sent from schools that I applied to began with the same message: "We regret to inform you …"

My move down South wasn't cashing in. I began working temp jobs and headed back to the place that I despised the most—retail. But I had to do what I had to do. I couldn't let the strong arms of pride choke me homeless. There was no pride worth defending when there was no food in the refrigerator. It wasn't fun to keep negotiating with my leasing office on when I would pay the rent. Through it all, I knew that things would get better. The only question was when.

By the end of the following year, I joined a mega church and became more involved with growing spiritually. I began to see things totally different in my life, especially with my relationship with Derek. There's just something about a church in the South. I heard messages like never before. Before being "washed clean" in the pool, I didn't recall days in early morning Mass like this.

The way I viewed it, my catholic upbringing was all religion. We went to church because it was what you did on Sunday. There was no connection to what I was learning on Sunday to how I was living the rest of the week, Monday through Saturday. Sunday was reserved for me not cursing or acting in an "ungodly" manner. There was no life-giving message coming from the sacred altar. Only chants and hymns in what sounded like a foreign language. Many of the sermons were call and response—the Father mumbled something, and we responded to it.

My perceptions about the good ol' foot stompin', hand clappin', head noddin' Baptist church were all wrong. I was converted from under a priest who sprinkled holy water on the congregation and burned incense to a bishop who taught his members how to take control of your life by changing your perspective. I transitioned from worshiping ceramic statues surrounded by lit candles to developing a deep understanding of the wisdom that came from the quotes in the Good Book. It wasn't just about the choir singing and the band playing. Members weren't using fans made out of Popsicle sticks to keep them cool. Now, people did do that fastpaced, fancy two-step dance they named "the Holy Ghost dance," but it wasn't just about that either.

First of all, I had never seen a fairly young pastor leading a huge congregation of followers before. His messages were more than just about giving hope. He made me believe that I could actually have a relationship with God. I began to think that maybe this was why I wasn't very successful in my previous relationships with men. As the bishop would teach, he would tell the curious members how our relationship with God had to be right in order for our relationships with men on Earth to be in place. There was actual meaning behind all this church stuff that I had missed for years. And there was something in it for me.

Every Sunday, I was a magnet to church. It's like I didn't know that I had been missing this part of my life for years. I longed to hear the purpose that I had in life. I knew that there was more to what I was living, and I finally felt like I was headed in the right direction. The church was a crisp, cool refreshing place that was teaching me about the wonderful life I would have by simply changing the way I saw all of the events that were happening or had happened in my life. Although, I was hearing golden messages of being prosperous and powerful, I treated it just like I did every other area in my life—a dream. I didn't know how to be a "doer" of the Word. I was so used to feeling good after hearing a message or wanting to make a change, but just accepting myself as never going to be different. I was new to this life and wanted it to dominate in every area of my being. In due time, I would be experiencing the manifestation of God like never before.

I remember one night at Bible study. Bishop called for everyone who was renting to take out a sheet of paper. On the paper we were asked to write at the top our old address and below it, the words "new address within budget." We were then instructed to fold the paper in half and take it down to the altar to be prayed over. If the church were a cult, I was all in. I believed in what God's Word was saying.

Exactly one year later on the same day I paid the earnest money on my house. God was real. It was a reality that He does make things happen. I just knew that He could make things happen in other areas in my life like love, but this manifestation wouldn't happen before experiencing the rejection of my new way of seeing things.

By now, Derek had relocated to Georgia. He noticed the drastic change that I had made in his absence. I guess he messed up by leaving me alone for a long period of time. Within six months, I was transformed. I started hearing these messages about being unequally yoked coming from the pulpit. This was the first time I had ever heard this teaching before. It couldn't have been clearer. According to the holy formula, Derek and I didn't match. We weren't compatible. Derek didn't attend church. He didn't read the Bible; he wasn't saved.

I was bitten by the holy bug. Everything that I was doing, I had expected him to do. Since everything else in my life wasn't going as planned, at least I would have some peace while I went through trying to figure out how things would play out in my life story. I had made a commitment to take this church thing seriously. As a result, my transformation affected the relationship that we had built together.

Anyone who has experienced getting saved can relate. You become so deep in the Word and this world of God that you lose touch with yourself. As the old church saying goes, "I was so heavenly bound that I was no earthly good." In other words, I thought everything that wasn't "God" was the devil. If you didn't speak the "ah sha tah" language, you were doomed. I wanted Derek to see things the way I saw it. Derek saw the change that I was making, but he wasn't ready to make the same life-altering decision at the time. My new way of life took a toll on our relationship. I tried to convert Derek by my words, not actions. As a result, he pulled further and further away from me. I began to see why there was so much friction in our one-bedroom apartment.

Within our small space, we used to argue over petty things. No matter what he did I found something wrong with it. He was the devil, remember? That's right, I blamed Derek for everything. I was unable to see my faults but could magnify his. I would turn a raised toilet seat incident into the Battle of Atlanta. The fact of the matter is we were two inexperienced individuals playing house. I saw us reacting to our issues the only way we had known—through violent words and actions. We cussed each other out, slammed doors, and hung up on each other—all actions sending a rippling message of "You just pissed me off!" This was so not Christian-like behavior. I would praise the Lord on Sunday morning and by Sunday night be fighting with my live-in boyfriend.

The secret lifestyle was starting to affect me. I felt like a hypocrite. Not only was I unhappy with my relationship, but I was being convicted about shacking. The sermons began to resonate during the days I trained myself to believe were not considered holy days of the week. The arguments were intensifying. I was trying to fly straight, and Derek was just trying to fly. Eventually I asked Derek to leave. His eviction would cause me to throw myself into the church even more.

As soon as I became a member of the well-known church, it was like I was being followed by the bishop. Every service was customized just for me. Surprisingly, each sermon focused on women and their choice of the opposite sex. The influential pastor began to teach the women of the congregation about what type of man a Christian woman was supposed to have. Ironically, I had just given Derek the boot and was open to find the man I was really supposed to be with. Out of the pulpit, Bishop continued to declare that a man and a woman were supposed to be equally yoked. I was just learning to interpret the Bible, so I may have been a little off with my translation. I took it literally. The man who had been in my life for all of these years wasn't "equally," meaning same or "yoked," meaning together.

No wonder it didn't work. I wasn't Derek's match. I wasn't the missing rib of his cage. We weren't compatible. Without realizing it, we had been forcing a square peg in a round hole for all these years. I began searching for a ministry to serve in and found my place in the one that represented who I was at this stage in my life—single.

PICTURE *Perfect*

The Singles ministry met every Friday night. My Friday nights would no longer consist of club hopping. While Derek was out shooting pool with his friends, I was attending church with other women proud of their title. I could relate to these women who had given up a life of sex before marriage and said "I do" to Jesus. I was sold. I immediately joined the Singles ministry.

I would receive more instruction on the type of man I was supposed to date by one of the church's ordained ministers. I figured that if the holy formula worked with homeownership, it had to work with relationships. It was time to rub the lamp and request a different man. I wanted a God-fearing man!

That's right! A man who attended church every Sunday morning and Bible study at least regularly. A man who held my hand and prayed. A man who took care of my needs, including the ones I didn't know about. A man who opened my door and sang that soul-stirring gospel music. Once again, I had no idea of what I was asking for. But the genie couldn't be biased, so he granted my wish. Now, I've played the secular game of dating, but now I had been introduced to a realm of dating that was all new to me, Christian style.

I began to look for love in all the places I knew of—wrong or right. The Internet was becoming a huge entity in dating, so I took a chance and joined an online networking site. I remember titling my page: *Christian Woman Seeking a Companion*. I was so proud of my new label that I wanted the world to know. Besides, I wanted to attract that man my bishop and minister had described so perfectly. Now I just knew that a man of God wouldn't falsify the Word! But when I tell you he left out the truth about the hunt! I sure couldn't say Amen about that!

Every man I met claimed to have had all of the characteristics that I wanted. In some cases they did, but they were truly missing character. I met the successful guy who claimed to attend church, but never wanted to go. Then there was the Bible-reading guy who only wanted to pray and host Bible study sessions at my house. He would later try to do some more studying in my bedroom. I have always been a sucker for good conversations, but these conversations were too deep. They had no real substance. They were, in essence, lame. They weren't fun. These conversational-type men may have been handsome on the outside, but they lacked a mental attraction on the inside. They weren't man enough for me!

Why did love have to be so ... boring? The grass sure wasn't greener on this side of the fence. I began to question myself. What was so wrong with Derek? I heard what my bishop was saying and truly wanted to follow his lead, but I just couldn't seem to shake Derek. He had a hold on me that was stronger than I could ever imagine.

For the first time in my life, I began to see myself as possibly getting married. But I didn't see myself with one of the holy dudes. If I were to marry this type of man, I would be doing so just to stay aligned to bishop's equally yoked sermon. In my spirit, something wasn't right. I wasn't happy. I was doing what I had been instructed to do, but didn't see the bliss in it. I was trying to follow the mold of what people had perceived a successful marriage to be. Regardless of how hard I tried, I couldn't settle. Maybe I had to be married to a deacon or become a pastor's wife to enjoy the happiness that I longed for. But none of those prospects were available at the time.

When it came to dating, church messed me up. For me, it was all about being saved. (I told you I was "Jesus.") I was so wrapped up in being a new creature that I lost touch with living with others. I was all the way in with no thoughts of turning back. I had given my life to Christ a few years back and was dedicated—to some extent—to living "like" a Christian.

After years of trying to find the man or even qualities of a decent suitor, I realized that church had its own definition of a godly man. What I couldn't understand is that if Derek wasn't God-fearing enough, then why was there such a strong connection between us?

Derek was street—simply put. He had a good heart and this is what I was attracted to. I had to seek God for myself. I would later discover that God doesn't look to see if a man ritually attends church, but that he has a heart after him.

Even though Derek and I had officially broken up, he was still somehow in the picture. I did feel strongly that he should attend church more. Like any sinner, he had his share of worldly problems. But in my case, I wasn't the problem, he was. Derek and I weren't making it because we were unequally yoked, remember? I went to church and prayed often, but was still following religion. There was no spiritual connection. There was no power. Derek didn't even go to church, so how could he spiritually be prepared to head a household. He didn't make a commitment to become a part of the church where I was an active member. He was a lifetime special guest or in other words, a visitor. He never prayed openly, only secretly.

I knew that I had tried to rid myself of the past. The Bible tells you not to "pour new wine into old wineskins" (Mark 2:22 NIV). I wanted to create a new thing, but didn't know that this could be accomplished with an old person. Although we weren't together, he had a genuine love for me that I couldn't understand. Derek hung around, even when I didn't want him to. He was always helping out. In the back of my mind I believed that if these other relationships didn't work out, I would always have Derek. I was trying to let him go, but he was somehow able to get back in.

Derek wasn't your typical "husband-material" guy. In fact, he was one of the many black men who we normally throw away. He didn't immediately possess the characteristics that bishop was describing. It was a process that had purpose and would take time.

PICTURE *Perfect*

REFLECTION

1. What is your relationship with God? How did this relationship begin?

2. What is your prospective husband's relationship with God? How did his relationship begin?

3. Do you trust God to develop the one you are dating or bring you the man of your dreams? Why or why not?

ALWAYS A BRIDESMAID, *Never A Bride*

"All married women aren't wives."
– Japanese Proverb

One by one, I watched my circle of five live out my fantasy. I was genuinely happy for my girls as they took their boyfriends to be their lawfully wedded husbands. Over the period of seven years, I played the role in one of their formal ceremonies. One, who I will call Rapunzel, opted to marry in a private ceremony with her pastor and immediate family. It was a quickly planned wedding; therefore, I had to support her from a distance. Ariel desired a small wedding party. As a result, I supported her on the third row of the deck that covered the bay. Belle was the first to have a semi-formal ball for which I attended to her every need. Both Tiana and Jasmine's wedding were by far the most elegant of them all. They both truly had storybook weddings. Tiana had two wedding ceremonies due to her cultural upbringing. It was like a scene from out of *Coming to America* with comedian Eddie Murphy. Nevertheless, I played my part in each celebration. Again, I stood by their side while one kissed her frog into a prince and the other prepared to ride the magic carpet

PICTURE *Perfect*

with Alladin.

Regardless of where it was, I supported my girls in their leap of faith. I didn't always agree on all of their decisions or their choices of men, but I knew how to play my position. I was doing what a friend should do. But as we reached this season of weddings in our early 20s, I began to question my own marital status. I was single. They were married. It was no longer me and the girls. I was isolated on the island of unmarried women, and I felt abandoned.

Deep down inside, I wanted to know when my day was going to come. For years they were everything to me, but in the blink of an eye some stranger had come along and taken their friendship away. My purpose in their lives changed from confidante to old acquaintance. I couldn't provide the intimate friendship to my sisters the way I once had. I was replaced by a foreigner and robbed in the name of "I do."

In some cases, the thought of marriage was simply by chance. The announcement of their special day came out of nowhere. In college we hardly ever brought up the subject of getting married. We barely even shared our dreams of no longer being single. I guess subliminally, the thoughts were always there, just never verbalized. That's why receiving the invitations in the mail or the out-of-the-blue phone calls were all by surprise.

After we all returned to our hometowns post-graduation, my girls began to tell me that they were about to be official. Immediately, I began comparing myself to them. Despite the story of two princesses, many of my friends hadn't dated their fiancés that long. Although the majority of the entries in my life story reflected themes of success: graduating with honors, buying my first home, and so on, the relationship chapter was still in the drafting stages. I had edited my version over and over but couldn't finalize it. And here they were entering a new chapter in their lives.

To top it all off, it was always consecutively. Each year was reserved for one of my girls to wed their prince charming. But I didn't know love enough to get married to it. I wasn't even playing the dating game at this point. I wondered what was going on with me. I was nowhere near the altar. There must've been something I missed in our crowded car rides to the clubs while drinking our cups of cheap liquor from the local gas station.

I started analyzing their reasons for getting married. For all but one, I understood why my girls, in some cases, rushed into holy matrimony. The pressures of having a baby out of wedlock for two of the couples forced their hand in marriage. Or simply believing that they were in love, or just feeling that they were ready, ran through the minds of the rest of them. I often wonder if they questioned their decision to marry their mate, because to me everything was perfect. Maybe that's why the expecting grandparents fronted the expenses of a quick ceremony. They wanted their princess to be "perfect" in an imperfect situation.

Nevertheless, they were married. I wasn't. They had accomplished every woman's goal in life. They had found someone with whom they could begin living their happily ever after. For the first time, I felt like I was unsuccessful. Despite me being the first out of the clique to finish school in four years, I was trailing them in my feat to snatch up a good man.

PICTURE *Perfect*

I believed that marriages were a reflection of the examples we saw growing up, in most cases, our parents. The same instances of generational baggage that our parents' parents toted are the ones handed down to us. The same problems we saw in our childhood home somehow moved under our roofs. In my opinion, my girls would have it easy, though. On an average, their parents had been married for 25+ years. They were protégés of a real-life union that worked. They automatically inherited the keys to a successful marriage. For their parents to have made it this long without any incidents of getting divorced there must be some power in this thing called love.

For me, the marriage that I witnessed resembled scenes from Ike and Tina. Love had nothing to do with my father fighting rounds with my mother. But in my friends' case, there was some essence of love. Their parents had the prototype marriage. I remember always admiring the fact that their parents were still married and for so many years. Their parents were holding on to something precious or simply just hanging in there for the sake of the children. Regardless, it was a beautiful sight to see.

But was it real?

I was the only one whose parents couldn't stand the test of time. For me, there was no design of marriage, only survival after divorce. Therefore, I wasn't supposed to get married, they were. It was destined for them to get married; they were simply following in the footsteps of their parents.

All of my friends grew up in a household of what seemed to be the picture perfect family. They took family trips, gathered for family portraits, and even were faithful participants of annual family reunions. To this day, many of my girlfriends' folks are still married. I wondered what they took from their parents' relationship that would either make their marriage work or mimic the lives of what they perceived it to be. Deep down, they knew the truth. But they wanted to hold on to their belief that marriage was a happy union between two people and that the butterflies would always flutter in their stomach. But the truth comes after a few years when the fluttering has stopped, and the challenge of staying happy is an ongoing adventure.

After I was captured in their fantasy wedding day, I played the single friend to the married women for years. Single ladies and married women play very different roles in relationships. If you think about it, they are either in one of two positions: longing to be married or having been there once or twice before. There is clearly a transformation that is made to the bride that takes place before she says, "I do," and is later cultivated.

Their conversations were different even though they told me that they didn't feel any change. In one case, the new life was everything that they wanted. One had found the perfect God-fearing man to share her world with. I remember her mentioning that she didn't need her husband but wanted him. With that response, I didn't know how to interpret her take on the whole concept of being married. Several miles away, Rapunzel was discovering that marriage was misleading and that problems lurked at every awakening. Arguing was a task that they faced quite frequently. The honeymoon stage was short-lived and reality would prove that it was time to go to marital boot camp, trying to save a marriage of less than two years.

Under the sea, Ariel was seeing how this new world was full of crabby challenges. Before even reaching the altar, Tiana, on the other hand, was fighting a battle of listening to her heart or following her family's tradition. Her marriage received a lot of unwanted input from outsiders who believed they knew what was best for her.

Then there is Jasmine. Jasmine appeared to be by far the most perfect of all of the princesses. She was a tall, beautiful model. She was always stylish. She and her boyfriend met during our days in college and were the only couple that I had known who lived the real college sweetheart story. They were inseparable at school. This wasn't a dude who I hadn't known before the announcement of getting married was made. It was someone who I had met, spoke with, and bestowed my blessings upon.

After graduating from college, a few years passed before they finally got engaged. It wasn't because she was pregnant. It wasn't pressure. It was for love. Let the fantasy begin! Their picture perfect day was truly classical. Jasmine and Alladin tied the knot in an elegant church ceremony filled with friends and families. It was everything you would describe in a fantasy ceremony. Her body was snuggled by the corset that I helped lace in her private bridal suite. There she stood in a white mermaid-styled gown that flared into a fishtail train. Her make-up was flawless—her hair elegantly draped back into a chignon bun. She looked absolutely breathtaking. I was so happy for her. As I stared in admiration, I knew that I would strive to have this day recreated in my own life one day.

They had no children and were an ideal newlywed couple. They had the house, the car, and a modest lifestyle. Their story read of happiness and pure bliss. As I continued to read the chapter, it would later reveal the truth behind their happily ever after. Within two years of their marriage, Alladin and Jasmine had become active members of newlywed boot camp and their magic carpet ride was about to end. I was confused. Now, call me naïve, but this wasn't supposed to happen to them of all people. They were perfect. Her husband who she thought she knew turned out to be someone totally different. No one saw it coming. Her reality revealed a living nightmare.

It was this example, and many others that followed, that would prove how marriage had to be created beyond the wedding day. I could no longer look at my girlfriends' relationships and envy them, or believe that I, too, would be faced with the same challenges that they experienced. But before I could become anyone's bride, I had to learn some not so obvious lessons from another well-known Disney character.

PICTURE *Perfect*

REFLECTION

1. Do you admire or envy your friends who are married? If so, why? If not, did you fully support their dream to get married?

   _____
   _____
   _____
   _____
   _____
   _____

2. How much influence has your dating, engaged, or married friends had on your desire to get married?

   _____
   _____
   _____
   _____
   _____
   _____

3. What discussions have you shared with your friends about being married?

   _____
   _____
   _____
   _____
   _____
   _____

DO YOU BELIEVE IN *Magic?*

*"Nonsense, child. If you'd lost all of your faith,
I couldn't be here. And here I am."*

– The Fairy Godmother

With one wave of a magical wand, Cinderella was transformed into a beautiful, elegant princess. The history of this tale is all too familiar. Many females strive to be the Cinderella, who in a matter of moments, went from rags to riches. Out of all of the characters in the story, it wasn't her mean stepsisters who helped make her into who she became. It was Cinderella's fairy godmother who served a significant purpose.

It was beyond simply removing her from under the strict parenting of her surrogate stepmother. The godmother was charged with providing guidance for the misguided "slave." She groomed her to be prepared to meet her prince charming. I love this story. It wasn't the part about the desperate girl waiting for the day her knight in shining armor came to rescue her. It was the magic behind the fairy who prepared her to receive her husband, the prince.

Even though the fairy was credited for causing the

PICTURE *Perfect*

most change, I believe that all women in some stage of their life are a Cinderella.

Although it is a fantasy, the story has some real aspects to it. I can say this because I, too, experienced a real-life fairy. The only difference was that my fairy wore a button-down shirt and tie, not a sorceress dress. Ironically, my godfather's actions were actually similar to those of Cinderella's wicked stepmother. I had to sweep my skeletons in a closet. This represented bad decisions and anything that I was ashamed of or that I struggled forgiving myself for doing. I then had to scrub the dirty areas of my past relationships, and wash my heart and mind clean.

He was sent to prepare me until my future husband arrived or until my existing boyfriend, Derek, received a major makeover. By this time, Derek was in and out of my life. My fairy godfather described our relationship as a dangerous situation. Mostly because we didn't know what we were doing as a couple or where we were headed. We didn't establish a plan. We had no purpose. We were playing Russian roulette with our lives. But God had a strategy for molding me into a prospective wife—my fairy godfather. My fairy knew the position that he was sent to play in my life. It took several years of disagreements and tough love for me to understand the critical role he played in my development as a woman and ultimately my future as a Mrs. After the time spent with my godfather, I was a new princess ready for the ball.

I met my fairy godfather at one of my temp jobs in north Atlanta. He was laid back, friendly, and extremely wise. He didn't walk around as one of those "holier than thou" church people. In fact, I didn't know for some time after we had met that he was a well-respected deacon at his church that later became my place of worship.

He approached me as if he knew he were on assignment. He saw a young woman in her early 20s wanting to know God in a more intimate way. It was a cry for help, though the cry wasn't verbal. It was sensed through my temperament and detected through my words. And just like that, I was taken under his wing like a fledgling bird. His role in my life was only for a season of three years. He was present throughout a lot of my hurt with men. One thing that he allowed himself to do was to become all things to capture one—me. In other words, he had the ability to become what I needed to develop me into a woman. He was a friend and a mentor. He was tough when he needed to be tough and compassionate when it required him to be.

But I was a handful. I'm pretty sure he wasn't prepared to deal with every dagger I was throwing at him. In one aspect, I was a woman with a lot of dreams. I was extremely discontent with where I was in my life and wanted more. Not just in my dead end job, but with men.

If I wasn't working in retail, I was accepting assignments through a temporary service. At the time, even working as a temp had me confused. It wasn't the career choice I had spent four years in undergrad preparing for. There was more to me than just filling out a weekly carbon timesheet that totaled forty hours for the week. I often questioned when my life was going to be arranged into what I wanted. From my career to my love life, I stayed on the prayer line. I wanted things to happen immediately. I wasn't patient enough to go through the process, but I was unable to settle where I was. I began to get a clear idea of where I wanted to be, yet the path wasn't clear of where I wanted to go.

Regardless, I knew that where I was, was not where I was supposed to be. As a newcomer to the church thing, I was trying to keep the faith, but I was too distracted by the things that weren't happening for me.

I remember crying out to God, "Please lead me in the right direction."

It's hard when you're a newbie to the saved life and are constantly wondering how God is going to put your life together. Since He was apparently on vacation and not returning my messages, I decided to make things happen for myself. That decision took me down quite a few bumpy paths. These paths brought me nothing but frustration and regret.

These unanswered thoughts had developed me into a woman of discontentment. My ambition caused me to make some irrational decisions. My fairy would get upset at a lot of the choices that I would make. He uncovered the scraps of my life, and realized that sewing the pieces together wouldn't be an easy task.

I was thirsty for love and was still in search of Mr. Right. I made some risky decisions when it came to the type of guys that I chose. The friction between my gentle fairy and I would reveal my hidden temperamental attitude. But anyone from the outside wouldn't detect this side of me. I would get upset when I didn't want to hear what was coming against a choice that I had made. Unfortunately, there's still a small trace of this trait lingering in me today. But I'm working on it. (This is good work.)

At that point in my life, I didn't realize how unprepared I was for everything that I had desired. After two years, the magical wand was waved again, and my temp job had ended. I would entertain a few odd-end jobs before eventually getting into my field of choice, writing. Within three years of training under my fairy, I needed more molding under his care. I didn't really know what my talents were even though I knew what I could do. There was too much doubt of who I was in my mind. I just couldn't understand why my life wasn't coming together into perfection. It was back to the drawing board. Not only was I wavering in my career of choice, but I was falling short of the qualifications necessary for being a wife. This Cinderella was failing. My friends had a lot of things happening for them. I wanted to see things working in my life too. I found myself always looking at other people's lives to compare my life to theirs.

The achievement that stuck out the most was that my friends were getting engaged and married. Relationships had become a sore spot. They stirred up so much anguish and disappointment. The relationships I had tried to force something out of brought nothing to me but tears and pain. I was constantly uncomfortable in this area of my life. This God stuff just wasn't working for me in this chapter.

Once again I took matters into my own hands, which just prolonged the process. I met a string of guys who I believed in, and it didn't turn out the way I wanted it to.

I would actually step out of the character that was being developed just to make things happen faster in my life. I was unable to resist the temptation of men. I was a "yes" girl to some extent. I wanted to please everyone. I would do things that I didn't want to do—all in my quest to be an item with someone. I can admit that I made some bad choices. I even entertained the interest of a married man. Even though nothing matured out of a few dates to the sports bar, never in my life did I think I would stoop that low, but I did. With other men, I took on their mentality, believing that I could have sex with no strings attached. I had a difficult time, and it didn't work.

My fairy godfather was always there to intervene. He prepared specialized plans to help me navigate through this uncertain time in my life. His lessons focused on creating a new mindset within so that he could groom me to be a wife figure. The magical "mirror, mirror on the wall" served as my daily guidance.

During this process of breaking and molding, I was forced to look deeply inside of myself. Before I did anything, I had to think about why I was doing it, what I was doing it for, or even why I was saying what I was saying. This road to redemption was extremely hard, as I felt God pushing His Word through the rock that shelled my heart.

I experienced random acts of kindness from my fairy that acted as chisels. I was given cards with words of encouragement at some of my lowest points. He had my back. I remember one of the cards having money in it to cover my overdrawn account. One piece at a time, a fragment of my hardened heart broke off, placing me at an extremely vulnerable time in my life. Through tears of disappointment, rejection, and being faced with the truth of who I was as a person, I was being exposed and becoming transparent. I was an open book—an easy read. The story of a single woman shared the hurt of my past and recovery to forgiveness. I never knew that I had so many issues that I had to deal with.

He helped develop me into the woman and wife that I am today. He was the first man to affirm me. I learned how to love myself first and then others.

For most of my adolescent years, my father was present in my life. His presence, however, lacked much of the nurturing that I was receiving from my godfather. My father was simply the male figure in the house. His relationship with my mother was one full of countless incidents of turmoil and injury. He was both physically and mentally abusive. I was so terrified of my father that him simply yelling my name sparked fear. I remember playing with my friends and being summoned from outside. As I timidly approached the screen door of our duplex, hurried thoughts flashed through my mind: *Did I clean my room? Did I take out the trash? Did I wash the dishes?* After conjuring up the best excuse, all he wanted was a glass of water. He was intimidating.

I can give him credit for one thing: teaching me the many things that I didn't want in a husband. From his actions, he made me desire to get hitched less and less. One thing was for sure. If I were to get married, it would have to be better than what he showed me it could turn out to be.

Now, I've heard that having a male in the household was beneficial to the training of males. Little boys must see a man in order to act like a man. Men are like coaches to their sons. Surprisingly the same is true for little girls. A father is the first husband that a little princess

PICTURE *Perfect*

has. She starts by learning to say "I do" to his leadership. He takes her through the dating and later courting stage by demonstrating how a man is supposed to treat a lady. The process is much easier when these values are instilled as they grow and mature. But this didn't happen for me. I was never taught how to be a wife through the direction of my father. He never took the time to teach me my role by example. This stage of affirmation wasn't experienced until I reached my early 20s. Even then, it was hard to accept this abnormal form of behavior.

By that age, I had already developed my perception of how a man treated a woman. I had allowed my negative experiences to mold me into the person I had become. Before my godfather threw a handful of sparkling dust over my head, he described me as being "rough around the edges." I had no formal training. I was mean. I was short in my words and snappy. The power of life and death does reside in the tongue, and I used my power for evil quite often. I was an unfit wife-to-be. There was a lot of anger and confusion in my heart. I often wondered why this life-altering individual was brought in my life. It was a higher love that allowed him to be placed in my pathway. Although my desire to be successful in loving someone and being their wife would take even more preparation, time, and patience, my faith in the process would be tested one more time like never before.

REFLECTION

1. Is there someone in your life who could strip you of your single habits and begin molding you into a wife? If not, where could you find that special person?

2. What individual traits do you have that need to be swept, polished, and cleaned?

3. What transformation will you make as a single woman to become a wife?

THE *Breakup*

> *"If you really love something, set it free. If it comes back, it's yours. If not, it wasn't meant to be."*
>
> *– Unknown*

I have never been in a fight before, but love has knocked me out a couple of times. No matter how good of a woman I thought I was, I wasn't good enough to be exempt from several rounds of heartache and pain. I've been hit with a combination of being cheated on to being misled. You would've thought that throwing in the towel would've been the best option. But it wasn't. I never expected the most dreadful blow of rejection to come from the man I spent the most of my time with in the relationship ring.

A broken heart can have you making some bad decisions. But when you find yourself at a crossroad or a desperate time in your life, you should measure your wisdom and not rely on your emotions. And desperate I was. I quickly shifted into protection mode and my guard that my fairy godfather had worked so hard to break down was back up. I resorted to my strong black "I don't need a man," female attitude. I even tried to get some tips from movies that supported this anthem. But

PICTURE Perfect

after a few times of watching *Two Can Play That Game* with actress Vivica A. Fox, I didn't want to play with my heart anymore. The movie was entertaining and very relatable, but my life wasn't a game. The rules of this dating game were too risky. I couldn't wait for him to call (as the movie suggested) because the tables would turn. I didn't want to be around my friends to keep my mind off of him. My heart couldn't handle any more advice from single, and in most cases, bitter women. I wanted to share my life with someone and create the love that I fantasized about all of these years. But I was too busy planning my day. With no shame, I continued my plan to get married, not in the future—but now.

By now, Derek and I were back together again. Even after my time with my fairy, I still didn't know why I wanted to get married. But at this point in my life, I was obsessed with it. All I talked about was getting married. I would start arguments behind whispering anything that remotely resembled the sounds of wedding bells. It was a subject that I had grown insane about.

Derek would never be the one bringing up the hot topic. It was always me pressing the issue. I took the bliss out of what was supposed to be a beautiful moment. Instead, my ambitions got in the way. It's like I finally wore him down to the point of pleading for mercy. I mean, after beating him over the head countless times with the "When are you going to marry me?" question, who could blame him. It was a slap off, and I was winning by default.

I remember daydreaming about the moment Derek would ask me to be his wife. On more than one occasion, Derek would claim his love for me, but fail to prove it with a ring. I remember one date night. We were waiting on a bench outside of Houston's restaurant. As we waited for our table to become available, an elderly woman came out of the double doors. She stared at us as if we reminded her of how she and her beau were thirty years ago. As the couple walked passed us, they stopped in their tracks and turned around. "My pastor will marry you," the woman said. Derek and I looked at each other in awe. She then proceeded to go back into the restaurant to get her pastor. This couple, who had obviously made it through years of the journey of marriage, had granted their blessings on complete strangers. The pastor came out and introduced himself to us. He then invited us to come to his church for premarital counseling. This had to be a sign from God. Things like this just don't happen without destiny being attached to it. That's all it took for me to turn into a woman on a mission.

From that moment on, I was just waiting for the day. We would be at dinner having a great conversation. I would picture it being the perfect moment for him to pop the big question. We would be talking about some general topic like sports, and I could picture him ending the conversation with, "So, what are you doing for the rest of your life?" From how I would cry to how I would cover my mouth with my hands and utter behind the cracks of my fingers "Yes," I would be rehearsing my reaction. The thought would remain just that—a thought. It's clear that I watched way too many movies. In reality, the moment would never come. Instead, another unexpected chapter would unfold.

The air felt different. You know how you can feel or sense that something isn't right? It was thick and uncomfortable. My baby blue walls that brought in so much sunlight would appear the color of indigo. I knew that something was heavy on Derek's mind, but to be honest, I didn't care. The sound bites of his words slowly drifted from his mouth to where I was seated. One by one each word traveled across the room penetrating my heart. I drowned out the truth as each dreadful word he spoke struck disbelief in my soul. I couldn't believe what I was hearing. "I'm not ready," he uttered staring down at his hands in disappointment.

My feelings immediately went into aftershock. It triggered flashbacks as multiple pop-ups emerged in my mind: The shipping of my wedding dress had arrived a few days prior. I had just modeled it for my hair dresser. (She had to determine how my hair was going to be styled for the big day.) Many of my word-of-mouth invitations had been confirmed. The date at Botanical Gardens was booked, and the deposit on my engagement ring that I picked out without him, was paid. I began replaying the annoying promises of, "I'm going to marry you." Derek had used my heart as a punching bag at this very hour. I couldn't believe this was happening. I was embarrassed. I was angry. And I wanted answers.

Women, in desperation of finally being able to call themselves Mrs., tend to ignore the signs that are so obviously present. I was truly guilty of the crime. I knew that Derek was doubtful about being married. But it wasn't about how he was feeling; it was what I felt I was entitled to. Just a few months before the date was set, I had practically placed a dog collar around his neck and pulled him on a manhunt to find the perfect wedding venue. I knew that I wanted an outdoor wedding, and the venue that I was considering received five stars from the people who recommended it. As I rushed to our appointment, I noticed I was the only one somewhat enthusiastic about the process.

We sat in the lobby as we waited for our wedding specialist to finish with a previous appointment. I grabbed a wedding album from the receptionist desk and began flipping through the pages. Derek's body language was screaming *I don't want to do this.* When our tour guide arrived, she immediately greeted me. She was chipper and extremely anxious to book a date for my wedding. I also noticed that I was the only one asking questions to the obviously pushy guide. I was the only one not seeing the $15,000 price tag as "too expensive." I was standing in the chapel, the place where we would wed in the event of inclement weather, and standing at the altar alone. All of these foggy memories became crystal clear as I tried to make sense of my world crashing down.

You mean to tell me after more than ten sporadic years of being his "wifey" and giving birth to his first child, that I wasn't good enough for him to marry? I didn't want to hear about the cold-feet syndrome. In fact, I had the remedy to warm up his feet! He owed me—big. I deserved the best, and he should've felt obligated to make sure I got it. But it was much deeper than I could understand at the time. I allowed the embarrassment and sting from him "calling it off" to cloud my judgment. He said he loved me, but if he really loved me, he would've married me. I know that everything happens for a reason, but this was that one thing that wasn't supposed to happen.

I was seeking a way to answer all of the questions

PICTURE *Perfect*

that were bombarding my mind. The intimate ceremony that took only three weeks to plan had come to a complete halt.

Was it something I did or didn't do? I knew that I hadn't intentionally done anything wrong. Quite frankly, I thought he was just being a coward. He wasn't being a man or living up to his responsibilities.

Just one month before, he had asked me when I wanted to get married. Now he was recanting. I never really analyzed the method in which he asked me to marry him. When I really think about it, there is a problem. HE NEVER DID.

Derek wanted to know when I wanted to get married, and I gave him a date. He never formally proposed to accept me as his wife, nor did we create the day or life that we would share after it. Instead, he was just trying to please me. To add insult to injury, he asked me over the phone. The nature of our relationship at the time, couldn't handle such an informal proposal. Since the birth of our child, our future as husband and wife was shaky, and I saw getting married as putting us on stable grounds. But I was wrong.

I am so thankful that he did call it off. I promise you that Derek and I would've been getting an annulment within the first three months—five tops. It's amazing how you never see yourself getting through a situation at the time until you are able to reflect on the blessing in disguise.

While I was the woman in waiting being pampered by words pouring from the altar, affirmed by the presence of a strong role model, and being loved unconditionally, Derek was in the streets. In his heart, he knew that he wanted to be with me. But if you recall, all of Derek's examples of relationships never included happily married couples. In Derek's perspective, marriage simply made things complicated. When people married, it changed the entire essence of the love that was being shared. It made the relationship too serious. And he honestly didn't want to commit to that.

I thought I threw away my impatient attitude with my fairy godfather, but I didn't. I was forcing Derek to marry me. I gave him an ultimatum about the direction that our relationship was going to take, and I didn't care how he felt. This was a big mistake.

If Derek was going to marry me, he needed guidance, not a threat. I was trying to take someone out of his comfort zone to explore a world that was unknown. He was being introduced to a lifestyle that didn't make sense. His perception of marriage needed to be changed. The day I was planning was all about me. I was creating a moment for me and everyone that I invited to enjoy. I neglected to focus on the person who would stand by my side after the wedding day ended. We both had our own perceptions of marriage, but didn't realize the power we had to change it. I was still operating off of past experiences and mindsets, and he was simply letting the image that others created for him to keep him from making a decision on which road to take: bachelor for life or husband.

"We weren't taught the following, …" I remember my bishop preaching one Sunday morning service. I thumbed the notes in my iPhone. "How to run a successful marriage, raise successful children, [and] handle wealth." It all made perfect sense. It's like the directions to obtaining these treasures in life were buried in The Secret (no pun intended). At the rate we were going, there would be no union. Derek was fearful of the unfamiliar and doubtful that it would work. We were at a standstill. I knew that something had to happen, and it had to happen now. If not, I was ready to walk away branded as a "baby mama" for the rest of my life. It wasn't the title that I knew I deserved, but I was at wits' end. Either that or our last names would be printed at the top of some court issued documents. I was quickly withdrawing my heart from the relationship, at least that's what I convinced myself to believe. I refused to waste another ten years of gambling on whether Derek would do the right thing or not. By now, I had crapped out.

It's funny how when you stop looking for something, you'll discover that it was looking for you the whole time. I had searched for answers and direction, but couldn't find my way. But it's something about putting what you desire in the atmosphere and remaining still. This time would be different. I had to trust that God knew where I was in my life at this very moment and that He was the only one with the answer.

From the depths of my soul, I cried out in prayer. In a matter of weeks, my soul cry was answered.

REFLECTION

1. What areas in your relationship have caused you to have any resentment or anger toward your man?

   _____
   _____
   _____
   _____
   _____

2. What red flags are waving in your relationship that you are ignoring?

   _____
   _____
   _____
   _____
   _____

3. Are you forcing your man into marriage or giving him an ultimatum? Why or why not?

   _____
   _____
   _____
   _____
   _____

BEFORE WE SAY, "*I Do.*"

> "Marriage is not to be entered into unadvisably or lightly, but reverently, deliberately, and in accordance with the purposes for which it was instituted by God.
>
> – Kay Cole James

An angel, with a passion to destroy the spirit of divorce, was sent to our rescue. He spoke with confidence and opened our minds to another level in relationships. Senior Chaplain Jonathan Grigsby brought light to a dark situation. Standing 6'2" with a solid physique similar to that of a professional football player, "Chap," as we came to know him, wasn't your ordinary minister. It's like he had his ear to the streets. He was a former womanizer, a divorcee-turned-happily married father, who was serious about his mission. Although his presence was to bless our relationship, he was particularly sent to save Derek from losing out on the most precious investment of his life: his family.

I knew I needed to be "schooled" on this new type of relationship I was seeking, but we both were about to embark on an intensive journey of understanding the institution of marriage. The same was true when I was

PICTURE *Perfect*

expecting our first child. I didn't know what to expect during labor and delivery, so I got a clear understanding before our daughter was born. For four sessions, I prepared myself through hands-on breathing techniques that I could anticipate using in the delivery room. In addition, lamaze taught me the technical terms the doctors would use. I read countless books and magazines on what to expect while I was expecting. I was now educated and had the power to create my own birthing experience. I began nesting the house by cleaning, purchasing clothes, baby furniture and accessories—all to prepare for the new bundle who would change my life as I had grown to know it.

When I taught seventh grade, I came into the school system with no experience. Although I graduated with a bachelor of arts in professional English, I only had the language arts background to carry me, not the classroom experience. After a short-lived career in writing, I knew that I wanted to be significant in this field. So now as a writer-turned-educator, this required me to attend seminars, numerous professional development sessions, and to eventually go back to school to ensure my credibility as a teacher. With a passing score on the certification test, I entered the teaching profession under a provisional license. The county, in which I taught, gave me five years to take any alternative route available to become a highly-qualified teacher. I then had to enroll at a university that offered my program of study. Again, I had some skills, but not enough to close the deal. I was a prospective candidate because I was taking the necessary steps to be successful. For me to obtain my certification would prove that I was dedicated, driven, and ultimately serious about my role as a teacher.

And guess what? The same approach was taken for my marriage. I knew I wanted this relationship to go against the statistics of it ending in a foreseeable divorce. If we can spend several years devoted to school, accrue thousands in loans, and strategically plan how to be successful in every other area in our lives, why wouldn't we do the same for our marriage? It's like going into business with a partner. Would you do business with someone who had no business sense? It's impossible to be successful and profit in something you don't invest in. Yet people spend several stagnant years in their relationship in default because a clear understanding or goal wasn't set before they exchanged vows or they failed to assess where they are and make the necessary changes to get where they want to be.

Let's think about this for a moment. The purpose behind any business is to create a product or service, and ultimately profit. Marriage can produce the same results if you go into the business of marriage with a business-minded person. It's not 50/50 but 100/100. The potential business partner or husband must bring all of his assets to the contract, or in our case, marriage license. But we all know that no one is perfect and business is never perfect, however understanding what your partner has to offer leaves room for improvement and growth within the years the business is open. In other words, you and your husband's qualifications are laid out on the table and goals are set. There's no fine print to read. You're fully aware of where your partner is before you went into business with him. You set your mind to plan and ensure longevity for your marriage. (Or this process will let you decide whether or not you want to get into a lifetime business contract with him.)

So, like my fairy godfather, Sr. Chap was specifically sent to prepare Derek for his role and he started by smoothing out Derek's rough edges. His delivery was simple yet profound. He was all about handling business and teaching the business of marriage. We knew certain conditions had to be in order before we uncorked a bottle of champagne, celebrating our new roles as husband and wife. Through the leadership of Sr. Chap, we were empowered to establish our own image of marriage. He taught us how to communicate with each other through the teachings of Koinonia. This new form of creating a relationship taught Derek and I how to have social intercourse, a practice we failed to establish effectively. Through Koinonia we shared our emotions, ideas, and anything that was of the present or to come. With this understanding, we took a closer look at each area of our relationship to see where we measured up.

I took on the role of student before experiencing the crowning of princess-bride. The living room of my suburban townhome transformed into a classroom of two somewhat eager students. It was like summer school for the students who didn't pass the state-mandated test. Retention was not a magazine clipping glued to my vision board; therefore, I knew studying, seeking the instructor for guidance, and putting my all into this experience would determine if I passed or failed. Through canceled sessions and being on the brink of calling it quits (more than once), I didn't know it would eventually pay off.

My studying involved a lot of self-reflection and evaluating. Premarital education allowed me to do something that I hadn't done since my days of Cinderella: look inside of myself. No longer was I able to pass judgment on my boyfriend and all of his faults. I was forced to stare at my thinking, beliefs, and previous feelings about what I believed a wife's role was in marriage. I was being deprogrammed from being single to being the best wife for Derek.

That's probably why I wanted to quit. I was never the problem; it was always Derek, but this unhealthy way of thinking would soon be rewired. Over the course of eight months, I discovered that my mindset about marriage was preprogrammed to the wrong channel. Not only that, but I didn't fully know the role of a wife. It was during our sessions that I discovered reality—I didn't know why I wanted to get married. When I thought about my reasons, they were superficial and fantasy-filled. I only understood getting married to be a task all females completed on their checklist of "to dos" in life. Maybe it was my subliminal thoughts and guilt about us being unwed parents and our daughter deserving a two-parent household. Or probably because it was the next chapter to our long-term, stagnant relationship. Besides, it was the "right" thing to do. No seriously, I had the foggiest idea as to "why" I wanted to link myself to the ball and chain like so many other unhappy couples.

But Chap saw a couple with much potential. He questioned our relationship and tested our strength time and time again. I thought even as an amateur that I knew what I was doing, but soon learned that the process of getting married happens in stages. This love thing was more complicated than I thought. The eight years we contributed was credited to our account, and Derek and I formally entered courtship. We were on our way to the royal kingdom in a horse-drawn carriage.

I heard my mother talking about her olden days of country boys courting her. This wasn't a modern term used to describe the hectic process of dating. I would discover that there was a pattern that people seeking to find a mate should follow. The key was the timeframe associated with these stages. Between dating and courtship, a couple shouldn't be together longer than two or three years. Derek and I were somehow exceptions to the rule and were trying to salvage the many years that we had spent together. I mean, I'm not the only one who felt like something had to come out of this time we invested.

Our chaplain would lecture us on the foundation of marriage and how to build our very own institution. Our two-hour weekly sessions of education and training prepared us to engage in a successful and, most important, happy union. Chap taught us how marriage is built on what he referred to as the "five core perspectives." With all of this, Chap gave us a new perspective on marriage.

In the five core perspectives (which I'll break down in a later chapter) married couples function properly when harmony and balance are evident in all of the areas. When we find ourselves having a breakdown in communication or not being on the same page, we would know which area is in need of our attention and how to address it. As actual students, Derek and I wrote notes from the sessions, had open discussions, and met periodically during the week to study the information we were learning. We understood that we were opening up our business tentatively on October 10, 2009, but there were still renovations to be made and inspections that needed to be passed before the cutting of the ribbon could take place.

Nearly a year had passed before we were given the blessings to officially tie the knot. This process sounds easy, doesn't it? It wasn't! Even though I enjoyed this "fresh manna" sort of speak and demonstrated my enthusiasm throughout this process, it was challenging and pushed me to think differently. It was outside of my comfort zone. But for my peer, in this case, my husband-to-be, I have to be honest. Derek only wanted to take classes initially because I wanted him to do so. But once he began to see the benefits and that there was something in it for him too, he started to shift his purpose for attending. After a few sessions, the lessons that were being taught about the Bible began to grasp his attention. He didn't realize how thirsty he was for the knowledge and through each meeting, Chap quenched his thirst through his unique style of teaching how marriage worked and was built on the foundation of the Scriptures.

It was happening; creation at its finest. Derek and I were actually taking the steps necessary to create a *Picture Perfect* marriage that would be like none other. It wouldn't look like my parents. It wouldn't resemble the couples' that Derek or I witnessed, but it would be customized to fit our picture frame. We had received the materials that we needed to strategically plan a life that we both could honestly say we were happy living in.

PICTURE *Perfect*

Before the contract was signed, we created a prenuptial agreement. Now, normally when we hear the term "prenup," it's dealing with financial situations only. This wasn't the case with us. The prenuptial we created was based on our relationship. At first I thought this was ridiculous. I couldn't believe it took this much to make a marriage successful. But then I started to replay all of the unhappy couples that stood as my example of happiness, so this had to be good work.

In addition to our premarital sessions, Sunday morning service was once again confirming where we were in our lives, this time as an engaged couple.

"People get married, and then they try to make their spouses live according to the way they were raised because they think that's right—instead of finding what God has new for them, venturing together and then building upon [that] … and the only way you become one is to come in agreement." Bishop was once again sending life messages from the pulpit.

It struck me suddenly. If we wanted something different, we had to do something different. It's funny how we had 10 years of off and on dating under our belt, but there was still a significant amount of work to be done between Derek and me. We needed to create a new experience with our marriage. And that's what we did. I made a conscious decision to prepare myself for success no matter what the cost. This was my attitude in everything I was confronted with, so I made a decision to have the same attitude about getting married and becoming a wife. We laid out the plans for our institution of marriage in our prenuptial agreement, preparing to make the ultimate business investment.

REFLECTION

1. What qualifications must your potential business partner (husband) have in order for you to consider getting married or going into "business" with them?

   _____
   _____
   _____
   _____
   _____

2. What goals would you like to accomplish in your marriage?

   _____
   _____
   _____
   _____
   _____

3. What skills do you have to sharpen before getting married and going into business with your partner?

   _____
   _____
   _____
   _____
   _____

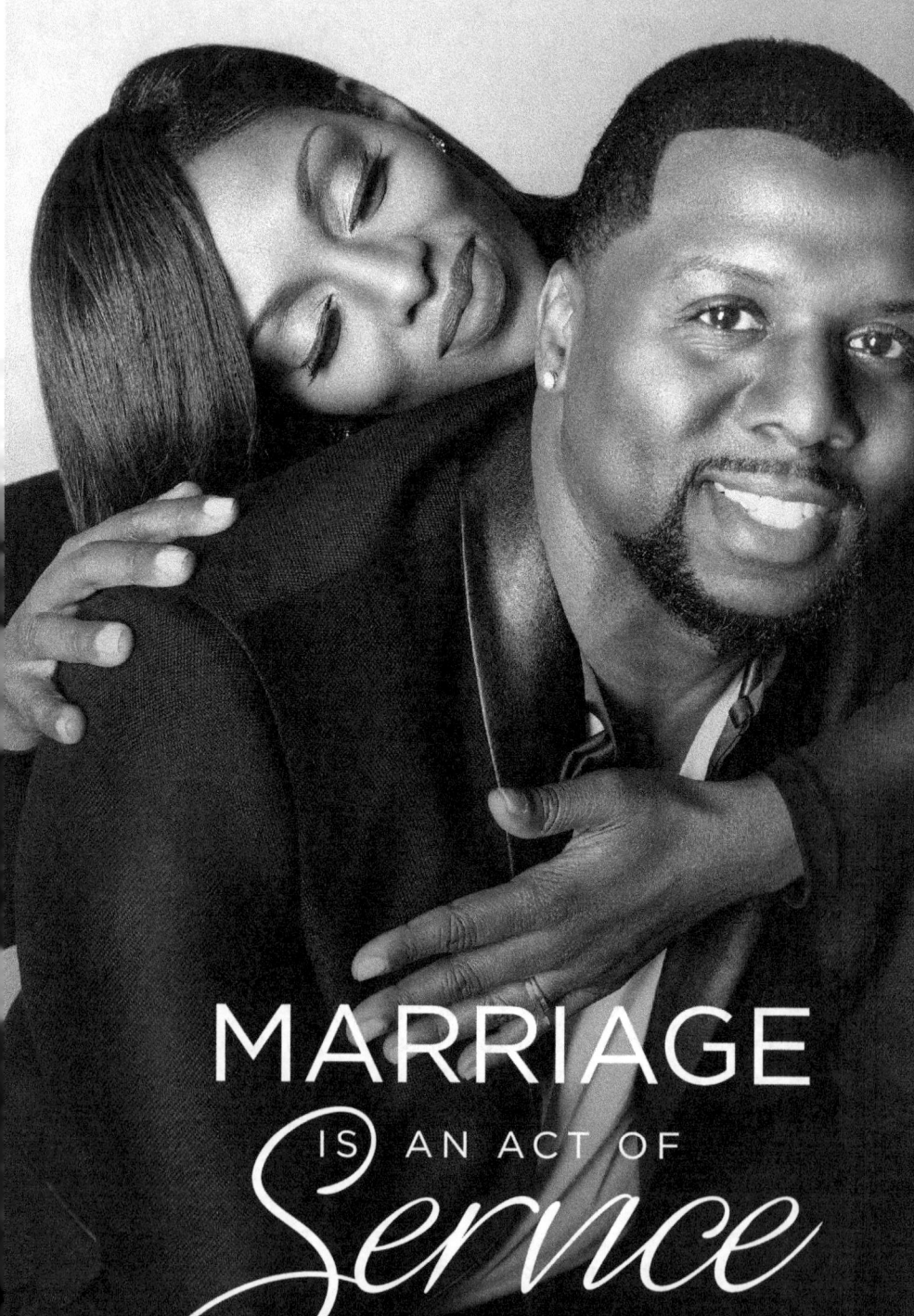

THE *Fairest* IN THE LAND

> "You come to love not by finding the perfect person,
> but by seeing an imperfect person perfectly."
>
> – Sam Keen

For years, I stood beside the bride in support of her transition to becoming a wife. With each wedding I was in, I longed to feel the joy of standing in her stilettos. I thought that if I was fighting back tears as a bridesmaid or in one case a maid of honor, I could only imagine how it felt to be the headlining act of the show. It didn't matter how traditionally big, culturally themed, or low-budget it was; I yearned for the day to feel that it was all about me. But I learned that it wasn't just my day … it was *our* day.

After three dress changes and nearly a decade later, the moment that I'd been waiting for had finally arrived. The tranquil sound of ocean water brushed gently against the sand. The air was filled with the sweet smell of summer's eve after the rain. The sweltering heat had subsided, creating a comfortable outdoor setting. In this story, guests consisted of onlookers and vacationers passing by to catch a glimpse of complete strangers exchanging vows. They literally stopped in their tracks to pay their respects to a couple taking a leap into the fairyland. Smiles graced their faces as they became a part of a special moment in life that many were all too familiar with.

There we stood under an oval-shaped gazebo made of white wood. Red carnations placed by hand on wild plants that outlined the entrance of the arc—simple but nice. On the sand, our family and friends created a hedge of protection just below the slightly raised structure. They traveled by way of passport to witness the union of their loved ones making a public declaration to become husband and wife. This was the moment I've heard about and imagined all of these years, except in this story, there were some modifications and revisions made to the blueprint.

Now, if you understand the history of marriage ceremonies, you know that all of the orthodox elements play an important role. You have the bride wearing something old, something new, something borrowed, something blue. Then there was the classic rule of the groom not seeing the bride before that special moment on the day of the wedding. Let tradition tell it, it was all about the ceremony rather than the role that the engaged couple were becoming. But tradition wasn't my reason for getting married. Thus, there was no need to follow it.

My wedding wasn't arranged, so no veil was needed to hide my face from an unsuspecting groom. Derek already knew what I looked like, so why would I hide my face? There was no classical church ceremony where my childhood pastor was present to officiate the service.

THE FAIREST IN THE LAND

The bridal party of the average six people, (who in ancient times served a purpose to confuse evil spirits) was nonexistent. The destination wedding gown didn't cost more than two hundred dollars, and daddy's little girl wasn't escorted down the aisle by, well, daddy, as tradition tells it. Instead, my mother gave me away. The truth is many of my extended family, although invited, didn't show up. It wasn't about the size of the wedding. It didn't matter if my wedding had three hundred guests or just us two. There was no rehearsal followed by dinner, no hostesses, no songstress, no piano, no dancers, and no programs. In fact, this destination wedding in the breathtaking Caribbean islands would prove to be far from the conventional ceremony that I had once dreamed of.

Walking on the matted sand wearing bare feet pearl sandals that hooked on my middle toe and latched around my ankle, I realized that the big, extravagant wedding wasn't necessary for us. Instead, the ceremony represented real love without the smoky mirror. Unlike some brides, our fairytale wedding only took five months to plan, not to mention a few hurdles we had to jump. I followed a tweaked checklist of what our wedding day should look like. In the end, we created a day that was our own. It didn't matter what critics would say or how they perceived it. The love we shared was authentic. We sincerely understood the transition that was happening. The bride was officially becoming a wife; the groom, a husband. The meaning of true love was definitely lingering in the atmosphere. Despite the frugal $3,500 budget spent, I still felt like an heir to the throne of royalty. This was my *Picture Perfect* wedding.

PICTURE Perfect

In an instance, the exchange of nuptials commenced. The minister, in his thick Jamaican accent, began to school two individuals on what marriage was all about. Little did he know the strangers standing before him were already aware of what he was lecturing. In fact, we had graduated from premarital education with honors months prior to this day. I know there's a prewritten script for getting married, but I wonder if men and women really understand what they are committing to do "Til death do them part?"

When I think back to the pledge that I was making, I can't honestly tell you what I said. I was in a trance. I was taking a leap into the controversial world of marriage. Regardless of what I was saying during the twenty-minute ceremony, one thing was for sure. The nuptials were already made prior to this Saturday evening service. I guess that would make it a prenuptial, huh? The commitment was inked privately before the production aired publicly. Again, this prenup wasn't financially provoked. It was the promise that we were pledging to each other. It detailed all areas that we would function from as a married couple. There were no fine lines or hidden requirements. Everything that was being presented to our audience on this day had already been etched in stone.

"The rings please ..."

Derek was directed to slip the diamond wrap that would complete the one carat princess-cut set on my finger. Simultaneously he stared in my eyes as he repeated the vows after the minister. Unable to hold back tears, this very moment was really happening. We were getting married. I broke down. This experience had overtaken me. I had awakened from my dream, and Derek was taking a leap of faith. He never imagined himself standing where his white flip-flops positioned him. He was becoming a husband and I—his wife.

We both glanced to the sky curious to see if fireworks would go off over the beachside. I know I expected trumpets to sound, announcing the uniting of royalty. But there was no manifestation of anything physical, just a subtle applause from our onlookers while the voice of Bob Marley seeped through the speakers of the radio. I entered the gazebo as Ms. and left as Mrs. There was a new meaning given to us. We had finally crossed over. The dream that I had always wished for had come true in real life.

PICTURE *Perfect*

REFLECTION

1. Describe your perfect wedding day.

   _____
   _____
   _____
   _____
   _____
   _____

2. Does the number of guests who attend your wedding matter? Who do you envision your audience being made up of?

   _____
   _____
   _____
   _____
   _____
   _____
   _____

3. What were your views on marriage before you tied the knot? After?

   _____
   _____
   _____
   _____
   _____
   _____

THERE'S POWER
In the "P"

"An excellent wife is the crown of her husband."
– Proverbs 12:4 (ESV)

There's a wise quote that says a man who finds a wife, actually finds something good (Proverbs 18:22). The last time I remember something being called good was when God made night and day. So, a woman is just as good as God creating the Earth? Now that's powerful.

But the role of a wife is above all things honor. To be called a wife means that you have been prepared. A wife has gone through the proper training to be able to pray for her husband and love him unconditionally. It involves more than just standing next to her husband as a trophy. She wears the crown. But this crown doesn't only represent her royalty or beauty. It signifies her position in this union.

Whenever I think about our classic fairy tales, the wife's role is watered down or underplayed. In reality, she plays a significant role in the marriage. A wife has the power to govern her house. She sets the tone, keeps the peace in the household, and is responsible for maintaining order. Her husband should feel this power when he enters his castle and heads the throne. A wife exerts grace and elegance beyond her clothes. Her beauty is transcended through her labor. She doesn't need cosmetics to create her look, only to enhance it. She is a woman of respect. She is highly esteemed and a woman of virtue. She stands as a protector of her husband, so he can fulfill his destiny.

It's funny. Everything I thought I wanted in my man would be my responsibility. All of these years I wanted someone to protect me when in fact my role requires me to protect him too. Protection would have nothing to do with physical strength. It was all in my words and actions. I had the ability to stroke his ego with words of encouragement, or strip him of dignity. Wisdom states that there is power in my words. Understanding that I literally had the power to win over my husband with my behavior was humbling. Although important to some aspect, the focus of a wife shouldn't rely on how fashionable she is, the diamonds she wears, or how often she gets her hair and nails done. Now, there's no question that a wife's appearance should be top-notch. But what allows the wife to win over her husband is her inner disposition. This is exactly why I needed the magical touch of my fairy godfather.

Notice the words of wisdom didn't say a girlfriend. I would come to the conclusion that we as women don't realize the power we have or the anointing that dangles over our lives. I knew that there was power in our "goodies," but it's deeper than that. Every woman has that power whether she is married or not. The real power, on the other hand, is in the wife and you deserve to be a wife of honor.

Late in our relationship, Derek began to refer to me as his wifey. I was honored, at first. To be called a wifey meant that this man saw me as marriage material. He could see me bearing his children. He could see himself "settling down" with me so to speak. But that was it. It was all a scheme to keep me around. As long as he could have me thinking that I was a prospective wife who made it to the final rounds, the relationship was perfect without legal documentation. He would never make it official. Why would he? I accepted being called his wifey. For some reason I believed that if I did everything a "wife" would do that Derek would like it and put a ring on it. I cooked, cleaned, ran errands, and gave him loving like only a "wifey" could. Not the case.

I began to come to grips with the term that meant I was respected for acting "like a wife." It wasn't good enough for me, but he was getting everything for free. It would cost to marry me. Not just financially, but emotionally. He would be committing himself to one woman, labeling her the highest position in a relationship, and unable to call it quits if things just didn't work out. Why would he do this if everything was going well with the wifey? Even my mother warned me that men didn't buy cows anymore. Women were happily giving the milk away.

Derek would never take our relationship to the next level. He was content with just playing spouses. But I was past that phase in my life. I knew that I deserved to be a wife, not just called one. Now when Derek first met me, I wasn't wife material—I had the potential. Through years of preparation, I became a wife, even before I signed my marriage license. I began to understand my power. Through my actions, Derek was covered. I stood beside, not behind, him as his partner. Together, we built this.

But although I held a significant amount of power, I couldn't overshadow his leadership. I was his wife, yet he was the head of the household. The last example of a head of household was my father. But I couldn't dwell on how he abused his authority at times. I had to know that Derek and I created a new thing for us. I had to relinquish my power to dominate in order to submit to his leadership.

Yup, I know! Submission is a controversial topic. A rule that women have been taught is that to be submissive to your husband, not boyfriend, is a sign of weakness. Submitting to my husband required me to let go of my independent reign and pass the torch to the man who would lead my life. In my prenup, I vowed to do the opposite of what I saw in unsuccessful marriages. I studied women and how they conducted themselves as wives. One of the areas that I saw a trend in was word choice. There is so much power in words. The Bible says that "death and life are in the power of the tongue" (Proverbs 18:3). In other words, I can speak a world of sunshine to my husband or create a world of darkness.

The sharp words that my fairy said I once spoke would've cut my husband—literally. I didn't know how to express myself when I was confused or even hurt. I allowed my emotions to overtake how I communicated with him. Whenever we had a "fight" or argument, I would've allowed my pain to build up and explode through, making cheap shots that would ultimately damage his emotions. If I was hurt, I wanted him to be hurt. Now, if I entered my marriage with this same methodology, it would've caused extreme problems in how we handled each other's heart. With my words, I actually had the power to emasculate him. The same strength that I wanted in my husband, I had the power to take away. Now what woman wants a weak man? As a wife, you have the ability to strengthen him in all areas by carefully selecting the words you choose to use. I rarely saw wives using their natural abilities with their husbands in a healthy manner.

In my *Picture Perfect* marriage, we both value each other's opinions on topics. I noticed how I spoke to him now compared to how I did when we were girlfriend and boyfriend. As a wife, I had to be supportive regardless if I agreed or not. We shared conversations, even when they were uncomfortable topics. I had to speak up (in love) when I felt that a decision he was making wasn't the best one. Nevertheless, he remained the head, and I submitted to his leadership. As Derek's wife, I helped him to create a vision for our family that he probably couldn't have created on his own. (I told you we are powerful.)

Since vowing to love my husband for better or for worse, I know why the conversation with my already wedded friends had changed. The expectations of a wife and a single woman were extremely different. Wives represent an elect lady. There's a different aura that beams around the woman who has made a pledge before God and her witnesses to step into her new position to become one with her husband.

PICTURE *Perfect*

REFLECTION

1. What is the difference between a bride and a wife?

2. After reading this chapter, in what ways can you play your position and be the best wife to your husband?

3. Describe what you believe your duties are as a wife, not girlfriend.

CREATING A HAPPILY *Ever After*

> *"Create your own magical realities and when truth comes and knocks on your door, you can invite her into your enchanted world."*
>
> – Sweetpea Fairy

After getting educated and trained on what it takes to have a marriage we were proud of, Derek and I believed we could create a happily ever after story. We thought about how we wanted to live as husband and wife, and took what we learned from our premarital sessions to create the vision for marriage based on some key areas. We looked at are spiritual connection *(We Are One)*; how we communicated with each other *(What Did You Say?)* and how we handled each other's heart and emotions *(It's a Heart Thing and No Love Jones)*. We then uncovered the truth and lies behind our finances *(Money Tales)* and how our marriage would run like a business *(Day-to-Day Operations)*.

In this chapter, you'll see how Derek and I came together (with the help of Sr. Chap's teachings) to design our version of the marriage we have today. I challenge

PICTURE *Perfect*

you to look at these same areas in your marriage and reflect on any necessary changes that need to be made. Remember, your marriage is your business. If you're willing to make the investment and devote the time and energy into creating what you want, your marriage will return to you a magical reality.

REFLECTION

1. Describe your picture perfect marriage.

2. What do you need in your marriage in order to live happily ever after? What are you willing to do in order to have it?

3. See your marriage as a powerhouse! What are your goals in your marriage? What plans do you need to set in place in order to accomplish these goals?

WE ARE *One*

Even before premarital education, I was developing a relationship with God. It took a few years, but it was definitely becoming a huge part of who I was. I was raised Catholic, so for me to separate the "R's" of rituals and religion was a deep cleansing process. I adopted a new "R" in my spiritual journey—relationship. I knew that a relationship with God was extremely important in my life. When I got married, I was a stickler on Derek going to church with me. It was the perception of what people would think about this. When I got married, the perception was still there until I addressed it.

I would often convince him to come to church so that I wouldn't be seen as a lonely, single yet married woman when everyone on my row knew that I had just recently tied the knot. If Derek was my husband, I didn't want other women wondering why he wasn't at church with me. I even found myself offering an excuse about him being out of town or having to work when I wasn't even asked. I didn't want them to question my marriage and who I had decided to make my husband.

Once again, I allowed the perception of others to

develop my own. I was a people pleaser and was more concerned with what others would think. This quickly began to cause problems with how we communicated with each other. I would get upset when I would wake up every Sunday morning for church. While I showered, Derek snored. I was disappointed. I would allow him not attending church to set the course of the entire day. I let not even the words, but the thoughts of some strangers to depict what I had created with my husband. I would hear my bishop tell stories about how his mother would win over her husband, his father, through her actions.

"... Be good wives to your husbands, responsive to their needs. There are husbands who, indifferent as they are to any words about God, will be captivated by your life of holy beauty" (I Peter 3:1).

Out of all of the notes I fingered in my note app, I didn't think that I could apply this particular one to my life. It was just supposed to happen. Derek was supposed to desire the same relationship that I had and he didn't. What I didn't know was that Derek was receiving his spiritual connection through me. *Pray for your husband, every day, all day.* This is the mindset I had to adopt, causing my behavior to change. I had to remember that I wasn't in this marriage alone, but with God being in the equation, I could now influence my husband in my position. Once I stopped nagging him on attending church, and began *being* the church, I saw a change in his response.

To this day Derek doesn't attend church every Sunday, but his relationship with God is growing. That's the point, right? It's not what others believe it should look like, but as a couple, we had to establish this understanding. And honestly, his appetite for a relationship with God has grown stronger and stronger. Sunday mornings weren't just centered on me getting up going to church. He began to get up on his own to join me.

We decided as a family that our spiritual connection was by far the most important aspect to our marital business. "We Are One" meant that we were aligned (God, husband, wife) which would give us the ability to successfully function in the remaining areas. If this pillar was intact, it would help smooth out the sections that we were still developing. But I still had to relinquish a lot of control that I had developed over my single years. Derek understood his newfound leadership skill and I was learning how to finally submit to it.

I stopped focusing on the tradition of going to church religiously every Sunday. It wasn't about that. I'm not saying that attending church is optional. We see the importance of having it in our lives, but you have to balance and decide how your marriage will respond to this area. I strongly believe that it's part of any couple's duties and responsibility to establish your expectations with attending church or developing a spiritual relationship with God.

PICTURE *Perfect*

REFLECTION

1. How important is it for you to attend church with your spouse or have a spiritual connection?

   _____
   _____
   _____
   _____
   _____
   _____

2. What role does God, the Source, play in your life? How can you ensure that He plays His position in your marriage?

   _____
   _____
   _____
   _____
   _____
   _____

3. Describe the trust that you have with God and your ability to create the marriage your heart desires.

   _____
   _____
   _____
   _____
   _____

WHAT DID *You Say?*

"It's not what you say, but how you say it."

Derek would preach this so much that I could anticipate when he was going to say it. With my mouth, I was spitting venom with the intent to poison.

I can't stress the fact enough. There's so much power in the words we speak. We can encourage or discourage with the same tongue. What an oxymoron! My words were sending death to my man—a man whose love I desired. Armed with my venomous words, I would strike whenever I felt threatened.

As a couple, we had begun learning how to communicate effectively. Remember, we both were rough around the edges, but I can admit that I was a little worse off than he was. I didn't know how to express my concerns or problems without copping an attitude. Even after years of preparation provided by my fairy and later our chaplain, I still had some traces of this trait. That's how deeply rooted it was. My fairy godfather always told me that my words were sharp. I didn't consider how the words that I spoke would be interpreted. I was always right and could justify why I spoke the way I did. I guess in my book if you said something that I felt was stupid, you would get cut. It was my defense mechanism. By taking this same approach in my marriage, my choice of words would cause puncture wounds. Eventually, my husband would bleed to death.

I believe my "switchblade" vocabulary came from my independence. The independence card was like a Catch-22. I had developed the mentality of not needing a man even though I knew that I wanted one. I had my own house. I drove my own car. I was a hardworking individual who didn't need a man for anything.

Can you scream "Girl Power!?"

I trained myself over the years to build myself up through my independence anthem. But during my wife-to-be training, this had to be addressed. I didn't know how to take the passenger seat so to speak. Notice I didn't say backseat.

Husbands and wives must be on the same playing field. As a wife-in-training, I didn't understand the impact this thought process would have on my husband. I didn't know how to talk to Derek or any dude who had gotten close enough to really see my true colors. He was beneath me in some sense because I had my own. I had a college degree, even though I wasn't using it—but that's beside the point. I was intelligent, driven, and didn't need a man. I was independent. And I was surviving all by myself.

Even after the fairy dust settled with my fairy godfather, that strong black woman persona was still lingering within. My word choice would be the cause of some avoidable arguments. When Derek would shed light on my shortcoming, I would be upset that my deep dark secret was revealed.

Constant arguing will almost certainly cause you to reconsider your status. As a married couple, we understand that there will be many situations that occur where we may disagree with each other, but we should be able to develop as husband and wife to a point where we don't allow ourselves to get angry. Anger is simply a red flag that covers up our true feelings. Instead of getting angry, I made a decision to get to the bottom of the problem. I had to learn to express annoying situations in love. Boy, did this take practice. And, honestly, it still does today. (This is good work.)

I didn't get it right on the first or tenth time. My vocabulary had to increase tremendously. As an English major in college, I thought I had a pretty extensive vocabulary, but it wasn't. My word bank was tainted when it came to the ones I selected to use, forcing me to think before I spoke. I realized that every word could either add fuel to the fire or extinguish it.

We decided to pick our battles because everything didn't require that much attention. I found myself speaking from my emotions. I had to practice honoring Derek through my words and actions. When I wanted something, I had to communicate to Derek and not expect him to read my mind. Communicating what I wanted in love (not attitude) was a task. I learned to love on Derek with my words. My words were sweet, and ego-stroking. Even when I didn't "feel" like saying those sweet words, I had to replay how it would come out before I spoke them.

After taking this approach, I saw a drastic change in

PICTURE *Perfect*

our social intercourse. We desired to talk to each other more and more. We opened up and shared our deepest dreams and visions with each other. He trusted me, and I him. It's amazing how powerful words are. When I was Ms., he never showed this side of himself, maybe because my selection of words always put him on guard. I wasn't protecting him, so he did what any man would—protected himself with a shield. As a wife, I made a conscious decision to choose the words that would build him up rather than tear him down. As a result, we're building an empire that's partly created on the pleasant words that we choose to speak to each other.

REFLECTION

1. What power do you believe resides in the words you use?

2. How can you train yourself to speak words that are pleasant and not sharp?

3. Create a list of words or phrases that you can speak to build up your husband.

IT'S A *Heart Thing*

I must've replayed "Emotions" performed by Destiny's Child a hundred times. I know that I'm not alone with this one. I would take the words from the song and use them to express how I felt at that very moment. No wonder I was depressed. I was truly lost in a song and growing insane by the moment. It was my emotions that caused a lot of my problems before I married.

Emotions can control the way you think or cause you to act foolishly. But according to Chap, only one-fifth of the foundation of a marriage is based on how someone feels. Many people get divorced because they don't feel that they are in love anymore or are having irreconcilable differences in one of the other areas.

Before we married, I was all over the place. My emotions would drive me into a state of paranoia. I was mentally scarred. I had been through so much with Derek that I didn't believe what we had was worth saving. My mind was set on him fulfilling my emotional needs only. I wanted to be wanted and adored, but I didn't know how to give it in return. We both had to learn how to love each other according to how we desired to be loved.

PICTURE *Perfect*

Derek first had to define what love meant to him. His definition of love was ironically different from mine. If I was going to appeal to his emotions, I didn't have to try and figure it out. He would verbalize what being "loved" meant to him. My duty was to take what he said and fulfill his needs. The same would happen to me.

Derek didn't understand the difference in how to treat and love a woman until he became receptive to the lessons of Sr. Chap. Chap showed him how to "pimp" a female from the right way of doing it. Pimping on The Fair Grounds was about having multiple women and learning how to juggle them all. Each woman would fulfill a different need for him. But Chap taught Derek how to appreciate having one woman who could cater to all of his needs. He also exposed him to the proper way to love me, his wife-in-training. Derek had to change his thinking and begin to not see me as his girlfriend anymore, but his wife. This new relationship between us was definitely a new picture.

Whatever Derek desires me to do in order to speak to his heart, I must fulfill it and vice versa. We have to desire to please each other. If we do, it will always be about the other person. It's never one-sided. Before I say or do something to Derek, I must see how it's going to affect the way he feels. Derek had to be able to trust me to never intentionally hurt his feelings. This would in turn build trust within our relationship. He could always trust that I would never do anything to hurt him, especially with the malicious words I used to use.

In any relationship, you have to make some decisions that can be extremely difficult. Without time to plan, life can present any couple with a fork in the road. The problem is determining which direction to turn. When it comes to decision-making, we agreed to not make ones that cause pleasure to our emotions. Emotions change. Feelings change. Something that may be good for us at the time may not be in our best interest to meet the goals and objectives that we have set for ourselves. It's all about the business of our marriage. We're in it to profit.

I finally understood the emotion card. At one point in the dating game, I couldn't convince Derek to say the forbidden three words. I guess that was one of the underlying rules on The Fair Grounds. You could never tell a woman that you loved her. As a girlfriend, getting him to say it was like holding his arm behind his back until he screamed, "Uncle." I once again won by default. But I wanted a true victory. I was so easy to say I was in love because like clockwork, my emotions had taken over. I held my heart in my hand—ready to turn it over to any prospect whenever I "felt" something. But the same man who dared to utter "I love you" to any woman other than his mother was now unable to stop himself from telling his wife how much he did.

REFLECTION

1. How can you protect your husband's emotions in the marriage?

2. How can you control your own emotions in the marriage?

3. Develop a strategy to ensure that emotions are not involved when it's time to make decisions.

NO *Love Jones*

My favorite flicks are romantic comedies. They seem to paint this picture that love is always passionate and lustful. Whenever a love scene comes on, suddenly I become hypnotized. I melt at every kiss, hug, and deep stare shared between the two love interests. It's like every movie would rekindle the dream that I held growing up. No matter what I was experiencing in real life, I always felt that there was hope. Someday I would feel this love that somehow only Hollywood was able to create. For the viewers, they weren't transmitting an accurate message. Reality would prove that this kind of love was hard to come by. The only way I could find this love was to go to see it in the movies, on Netflix, or rent it from Redbox.

In my fantasy, I would find this hopeless romantic who sent chills up my spine at every encounter. He would kiss me oh so gentle, sparking electricity through my soul. I would tingle at every touch and yearn for him to make passionate love to me. I wanted to not only love my man but, most important, I wanted to be *in* love. I found out that I was in love with the thought of being in love. I thought the main reason for getting married was for love. That was the common theme in all of the stories. But there is much confusion with this term. How can you get married for something you have no idea about? Sadly, it happens every day, mostly on Saturday evenings, the most popular day to get hitched and most profitable day for the venues.

So, what is love? Love is first a decision. I was under the impression that love was something that just happened. I didn't realize how much "free will" we had in choosing to love or not. But with age comes wisdom. All I had to offer Derek were my raw experiences with past relationships. They say experience is a good teacher. At the time, I would've strongly disagreed. I was taught all of the negative sides to that precious word *love*. Love taught me to be bitter. It taught me that "men were no good" as I was warned so many times before. It also taught me to grow a third eye, because trusting the opposite sex was like walking across the street without looking both ways. Eventually, you would get hit! (I guess you can say, love was dangerous too.)

Over the years, I just knew that I was in love with Derek. Now my definition of being in love was taken from the scenes in the movies. I would wait by the phone contemplating on calling him or waiting to see if he would call me. We would spend hours talking on the phone throughout the night. I never wanted the night to end. Not to mention, thoughts of him ran through my mind the next day, all day. I was head-over-hills for some Derek. But this emotion would come and go. It seemed stronger when we were dating. Again, I was in love with the thought of being in love.

I've discovered one truth. To love someone you must

know what it means to them. You can only love someone according to their definition of love. What I later learned was that Derek must feel that the love I have for him is literally his. The type of love given to me by Derek gives him the power to be the man I needed and wanted him to be. This would grow our love for each other. I made a decision. I wanted to feel love so badly. Sadly, I didn't know that I had the power to create it.

It took a few trips and scrapes on the knees before I discovered the true meaning of "falling in love." I really don't believe in falling in and out of love. To fall in love means you involuntarily made a decision to show affection toward someone. Remember, love is a decision. It's something you can choose to do or not. Therefore, falling in and out of love is a choice. Even in the make-believe world, prince charming and his princess made a decision to love each other. And they apparently didn't have much history together. At first, love for me was Derek being able to read my mind. He should've known how I was feeling and immediately had a solution to fix it. If he loved me, he should've known that I loved spontaneity. But I was setting myself up for failure. Not only was I unaware of what love I wanted, neither did he.

When we married, I can't honestly say that I was "in love." By the time we had successfully made it to the altar, I had made a decision to love Derek according to what he defined love to be. Before this point, I didn't fully understand how to love my man. I believed that my man was supposed to be deeply in love with me. In fact, I believe some female with good intentions told me that he was supposed to love me more than I did him. I'm assuming that she was just trying to figure out

PICTURE *Perfect*

a code for any fool wanting to be loved. I honestly believed this mentality and brought that same mindset to my premarital sessions.

I tried every example known to man and discovered that the first example of love is God. Love is patient. Love is gentle. Love is kind. (1 Corinthians 13:4) When you marry, husbands are told to love their wives like Christ loved the church. Now I had no idea what this meant. Jesus was an exception to the rule. I had to look at love and see what it was that I needed. Most people don't look at love. I had to evaluate all of the sacrifices that Derek made and the love that he executed.

Likewise, I had to learn to define my love. Anytime something is important to me, it falls under love. I never wanted to manipulate love to control Derek, but I knew I had in the past. Once I understood how to love Derek according to his personal definition, I then turned to the biggest part of physical love in a marriage: sex. This was yet another fantasy that I had to make into a reality.

I was under the impression that the moment you say "I do," your desire for sex was supposed to intensify. Traditionally the honeymoon is a time when intimacy is at its peak. The couple sets the course of what their consummating act (which most of the time happened long before the wedding day) will look like post-wedding day. If this is any indication of what sex after marriage will be like, people wouldn't get married for the lack of sex alone. I always wondered why people would say, not too long after their wedding day, that the honeymoon was over. I guess the couple was in temporary marital bliss because they were in paradise continuing part two of the wedding. Their honeymoon was full of affection, love making, kissing, and a euphoric feeling that made them believe that sex in their marriage would forever be amazing. Once again, there's some hidden truth to this fantasy world.

Sex was a hobby that Derek and I enjoyed from the moment we were an item. It was good—real good and plentiful. It was nasty, and I craved it (he did too). I was a bona fide member of the late '80s R&B group Vanity 6. As singles, you couldn't tell us that we didn't invent sex. Our sets changed more than our positions. We were exploring every way to make sure that the neighbors knew our names. Okay, maybe I'm exaggerating a little, but sex was really fun. However, this exotic scene would soon change. When Derek and I had made a decision to love each other and take the necessary steps to build the foundation of our marriage, I truly wanted to take the focus off of sex and concentrate on working on us without being distracted by lust. Sex, although a large piece of the love-relationship puzzle, can cause anyone to lose focus on their intentions.

My intention was established. I wanted my marriage to work, and if sacrificing sex for a few months would help ensure a happy marriage, I was willing to do that. Derek, on the other hand, was totally against that reasoning. Even though he and I were preparing to be together forever, he didn't see the logic in making him wait until our honeymoon. As our premarital educator informed us, I desired the blessing of having "fireworks go off in the bedroom." I was told that by holding out before the wedding, I was setting myself up to turn my husband out sexually.

I guess I didn't really understand what that meant.

PICTURE *Perfect*

I took him for his word and convinced my frustrated husband-to-be to wait. I wanted our sex life to be perfect, but our minds had to be renewed as husband and wife. I wasn't created to perform sexually as a wife. I had been a girlfriend to Derek for so many years that we had to create a new sex life too. Now, I still held my own. But I was still longing for it to resemble the passionate love scenes I had seen on television.

I would come to find that married couples—the elite, the crème de la crème—aren't even having sex. The only cooking that's happening is in the kitchen. And that's barely hot. The bedroom is going through withdrawal. It has resorted to a place of resting. There's no passion. There's no excitement. It's boring. There was more 12-Play happening when they were dating without a plan or purpose. It's like the moment the ring was slid on the finger, it sent a message to the heart that things were going to get real ritualized. The world they live in becomes mundane. Their days consist of getting the kids ready for daycare or school, going to work, coming home, fixing dinner, and getting ready for bed. It's this same routine that makes marriages become old and stale. And we didn't want this.

The spark that kept them tingling inside is flickering. I don't get it. When you're married, you basically have permission to have your way with your spouse, but we were having more fun as singles than being hitched. The bed was supposed to be a picture perfected with uncut, raw action. It's funny how we were illegally having sex, so to speak, as a single couple, but we weren't taking advantage of it as a married couple. To add insult to injury, I would throw that same fantasized picture in

Derek's face. We couldn't have wild, dirty sex until we were "made right before His eyes." Even though he had seen every piece of my birthday suit, he needed to wait. I wanted to wrap myself up again to be the gift that he would unwrap on our wedding night. Now that he had made me an honest woman, what was my excuse now?

Aha, yet another part of the story that was left out. My desire for sex initially declined. The hustle and bustle of everyday life would have an adverse affect on my drive. I was performing well with keeping up with our toddler, attending class, and completing all of my assignments on-time. Every Sunday, I was working on my lesson plans for the school week, but I was never planning how to perform for my husband. But why was I the only one affected? Derek's sex drive has never been affected—ever. I just figured that he was supposed to understand that life had so much on my plate that I didn't have room for dessert. I was stuffed with priorities that I made him secondary. I was neglecting my business or marriage at home.

Derek would always remind me that I was playing multiple roles that required an equal amount of attention. I would always be a mother. That would never change. At this point in my life I was a student and teacher. Until I finished, it was an active role in my life. Not to mention, most important, I was a wife. I had to find balance.

I began thinking of creative ways to give him his "quality" time at home. It began with prioritizing. I wanted the bedroom to be electrifying—a place that changed the mood of how I was feeling. But it didn't have to stop there. We had to get creative. I prayed.

PICTURE *Perfect*

Nothing. The spark was still dying out.

I did my best to hold out during our premarital education but once again, I was sold a dream. You would think by now I would ask more questions than just believing another sales pitch. It wasn't until I renewed my mind about sex that the lights, camera, action turned on and it was showtime. I was putting so much time and energy in my personal life that I forgot that my individual life was now conjoined with another. I was spending extra hours at work, devoting time to extracurricular activities, and realized that I was doing too much during the day.

By the time I got home, I had nothing to give to the most important person in my corner—my husband. I started understanding why my libido was low. I wasn't being affectionate with my husband. Before we went our separate ways in the morning, I didn't give him a hug and kiss that would have me on his mind the entire day. When he came home, I wasn't stopping what I was doing to make him feel that he was just that important. I just expected it to happen. I decided to do something out of the ordinary. I admired the love scenes so much that I had created my own. I took him by surprise when he came home and saw me all dressed up in character.

Everything that made me tingle in a movie was being previewed in my bedroom ... well in the living room first. I found myself doing everything that I wanted him to do to me. I began whispering in his ear and kissing his neck. I even started cuddling on the couch while we watched television stroking his chest and lower abdomen. Before I knew it, my sex drive went into overdrive. My prayers were answered. See, I just prayed and expected it to happen. What was missing were my actions. I had to create my sex life. When I mentally created a concept of what it looked like for me, I was able to take that vision and design my own sexual healing.

The cure: I was still trying to function under the "girlfriend" mode, not operating as a wife. Derek and I kept trying to relive our times when we were young and experimental. We kept trying to recreate the old instead of creating something new. I sought to please Derek in every way possible. I noticed that as I pleased him, he sought to please me too.

PICTURE *Perfect*

REFLECTION

1. What has helped you to make the decision to love your spouse? What does that love look like?

2. How important is sex in your relationship for you and your spouse? Why?

3. What can you do to make your fantasy sex-life or favorite romantic movie scene a reality in your marriage?

MONEY *Tales*

The old adage says that money can't buy you happiness. Well, I say that it may not buy happiness, but it sure puts a down payment on it. When your finances are in order, you have more freedom in your relationship to focus on what really matters: love. As a wife, I'm starting to understand the real purpose for money. Money equals endless possibilities. It opens shut doors, or it'll buy you a door to open yourself. The power that money brings is immeasurable. But there's a catch. You have to know how to manage it—not to mention develop a healthy relationship with it.

Any married couple knows the power that money brings to their relationship. Having a substantial amount of money (the amount varies for each couple) will position them into a realm of financial freedom. The liberty to explore all of life's hidden treasures will be afforded to this couple all because they have access to this tool. The burden of having no money creates problems that can lead to addictive and destructive habits. You can have every good intention to have a successful marriage, but if your finances aren't in order, you will realize that the spouse you attached yourself to may be deep in debt

PICTURE Perfect

which equates to tension, unhappiness, and resentment.

Now some of you may be reading this in total disagreement, and that's okay. It's such a contradiction when people who don't have money say it's not everything. I'm simply implying that when it comes to a lifetime partnership, it plays an important role. Money is needed for everything we do in our lives. Anything from filling up your gas tank, purchasing food and clothes, and paying your mortgage—money is the common denominator. This doesn't mean that the focus of the relationship will be on money or that you should begin worshiping it over your spouse, but it does mean that you can't ignore the role it plays in any relationship. Research shows that at the center of many divorces the "lack of money" or financial problems has shown its piercing face.

One thing's for sure—even in our make-believe stories—prince charming approached his potential bride with money. He was royalty. Money automatically was his inheritance. This is probably why their love appeared to be so easy. You never saw the couple in these stories arguing over finances. You never read about the couple living check to check just to make ends meet. It was obvious that money was an integral part of the equation.

I don't believe that money solves every marital problem. There just has to be a balance in your overall business plan. I often wonder if couples with endless cash flow will still be in love if their money ran out. Many people may disagree with this, but love is easier when plenty of money is involved. When it's scarce, however, the problems start to occur, or the meaning behind true love is exposed.

From a young age, I always knew that saving money was important. As kids, my sister and I shared a large, pink piggy bank that we used as our bank account. Our parents instructed us to place all of our change in it. Mostly pennies and on a good day a few silver coins were inserted in the slot on the back of the ceramic swine. The myth behind the collection of coins was that it would be used toward college. That goal seemed so far away and unobtainable. The truth was that the pig would later be broken into for an early withdrawal. Over a period of time, the coins were used for the ice cream truck, school lunch, and other purposes. My piggy bank was my first experience of failure at saving money. My second fate presented itself in the form of bonds. My father used to purchase savings bonds through his Postal Service job in increments of $25, $50 and $100. By now, the piggy bank was slaughtered. I had nowhere to deposit my paper money.

I remember storing my bonds in the inside cover of an encyclopedia on my desk. The bonds were definitely an upgrade from the outdated piggy bank savings. If the bonds matured over the years, I would receive the face amount. However, if they were cashed prematurely, they would only be worth $25 regardless of the amount of the bond. Unlike the piggy bank, this money wouldn't be easily accessible. It had to be cashed at an actual bank. I had every intention to see my bonds grow up. But which option do you think was modeled for me? It wasn't my addiction to sunflower seeds and pickles that made me broke this time—instead, my father's unknown drug addiction. Since the bonds were made out to me, my signature was required to cash them. I would,

PICTURE *Perfect*

under the pressure of my father, sign over my bonds. The bonds that I collected were quickly cashed, leaving me with yet another depleted "college" savings.

Savings for my mother came in another form. The only saving I witnessed my mother modeling was an attempt to save our home and, at one point, her marriage. Not only was her relationship with my father strained, but there was never a good understanding with money. Uncle Bill and Aunt Debt ruled the household. Opening bills was like a secret ritual. I would never see my mother face the fact that she owed people. The word "bill" had a negative connotation attached to it. We never spoke about it. But we did know that our family owed something to somebody. I remember the phone ringing throughout the day. The pressure of owing really took its toll. Fear had overtaken our lives so much that when the phone rang, we took cover. We treated bill collectors like Jehovah Witnesses—we hit the floor, remained silent, and hid until the phone stopped ringing. When I did answer the phone, because my mother refused to face the music, I would lie and say that she was unavailable.

For the majority of my childhood, my family consisted of my mother, father, older sister, incarcerated brother, and Aunt Debt. Having money was a scarcity in my household, especially after my parents divorced. After living that death experience, my example of spending money was simple: always wish for it, but never expect to get it. We could never get ahead. Mother would put her chances of winning it big in the lottery or playing bingo to get us out of our slump. "Win something," I declared as I kissed her goodbye, leaving her with those two words of good luck. She would go to the bingo hall or the basement of a neighborhood church and set up her table with dozens of bingo cards surrounded by the magical troll dolls to increase her changes of winning. Sometimes she would win; sometimes she wouldn't!

My mother worked like any other single-parent divorcee raising a family. She slaved forty hours weekly in addition to working overtime. All of her hard work never seemed worth it. I never saw her have anything for herself. The extra money she would get from overtime or her sporadic winnings would go to us—her girls. She taught me through her struggles with finances that you have to sacrifice. But sacrificing meant that you would never have any money. I hated the mentality of living paycheck to paycheck. I wanted to be rich because not having money created so much bondage.

The purpose of working became solely to pay the bills, but even that wasn't enough. We either needed to add more hours to the day or she had to get a second job. My mother chose the latter. Managing a local pizza store in addition to her 9-to-5 still couldn't bring one end to the other. Poor Paul was robbed every month to pay Peter. If one bill was paid, one was neglected. It was a debate of how to spend the limited funds. That debate would always leave Paul's cousin unpaid too. I remember when the gas was turned off several times. The choice to pay the electric over the gas made more sense. Bath time consisted of heating up water in a big silver pot used to cook collard greens or boil potatoes. I would wake up at least two hours before school to preheat the electric plate. Cold running water would be added to the boiling water to make a somewhat comfortable bath.

PICTURE *Perfect*

Thinking back as a child, I never understood how people worked forty hours a week and were still broke. But this was my reality. Once I left the household that practically raised me—not trained me—my vision was misconstrued. I was sent out in the world not knowing how to handle my finances. I saw the struggle that my mother went through both financially and in relationships, but I was inexperienced and in many ways reckless in handling my life. I subconsciously packed the same broke mentality of my parents and took them with me. Within my first year in college, I applied for my first credit card. With no job, and no proof of income, I was granted a $1,000 limit. What other way to spend the money that was granted to me than to go shopping. Plus, I received a large refund check from school so I thought I was doing pretty well for myself. This was the beginning of my end for Aunt Debt had followed me for the next ten years of my life. To this day, I'm still paying for that shopping spree (too bad I don't have the clothes to show for it) and setting up extended forbearances for my student loans.

About five hundred miles south of Maryland, Derek was dealing with the same factors. He had his mind on his money and his money on his mind. Money was always a problem in his household too. No one ever had enough to do anything. It was always a need: "I need to pay this." "I owe this." "I ain't got this." "Can I hold something?" "What you got for me?" were usual greetings during a main conversation.

The hustle mentality began with selling candy to students in school. Derek knew that once he made the money, no matter what happened, he could always make it back. He would multiply a single purchase of a box of Debbie Cakes, M&Ms, Twix and other chocolate delights that kids go crazy over. The royal wardrobe was purchased through the profits that were made from selling candy. Of course this budding entrepreneur's newfound fortune was hidden from the circle of females in his house. Derek was in many ways like the late rapper Biggie Smalls. He used to leave the house wearing the hand-me-downs and Goodwill gear that his aunts worked so hard to get, only to sneak behind the trailer to change into his brand new Air Force One sneakers and Polo apparel. Seeing how much money he was making, the desire to make more led to larger transactions.

When I think back to the example of marriage with my parents, money was one factor of why they didn't make it. Money is so important, yet we shy away from fully addressing this topic. Either you have it or you don't, want it or can't get it, know how to manage it or not—no matter what, you need it.

When Derek and I were preparing for marriage, we immediately discovered where our challenges were: finances. It was like a weed had been sent to destroy every happy flower that had grown in our life. We both, coming from two different backgrounds, had different perspectives on money. Actually, we had more in common than we thought. We both were unfaithful when it came to money. It went from one extreme to the next. We used it. Lied to it. Abused it. Raped it. You name it. We both developed destructive relationships with our money at a young age and were bringing these same habits into our marriage. It wasn't long before Round 1 began. Let's get ready to rumble.

PICTURE *Perfect*

I, being financially incompetent, depended solely on his experience and knowledge of how to handle money. As a master barber, Derek was used to making fast cash. Just as fast as he made it, he would spend it. Finances is one of the leading reasons why married couples divorce, so we had to develop a plan. There had to be something that we could do to heal our torn relationship with money. I had to begin with how I saw debt. The thought of owing anyone would make my heart race. I saw what debt did to my parents' relationship, and I was fearful that the same hook would snag us out of happiness. There was no liberty in always owing someone. I just knew that I had to re-evaluate how I saw money and began working toward making up with it. (This is good work.)

I started by truly understanding the tool that money is in my life. In order for me to have the freedom to do the things necessary and desired, I had to have a strong, healthy relationship with it. It all started with me consciously changing the names that I used. The words bills and debt had to be removed from my vocabulary. There was such an uneasy feeling related to each word. Plus, my history with the two painted a picture of deceit and misuse. The negative connotation associated with these words made me start calling "bills" and "debt" simply my expenses. It sounds like a simple change, but it transformed the way I thought about paying someone I owed. I didn't feel as if I were in any form of confinement. I was handling business like a business-minded person.

To discover how much currency was flowing in and out of our household, we developed a plan of tracking our spending. During my early years of adulthood, I was irresponsible with money. Even though the bills were paid—sometimes on-time and others through arrangements—I still mismanaged my income. Every time we spent money, we had to track it in our phone. To both of our surprise, we began to see how we really are millionaires with a poor man's mentality. Over the course of weeks, what we were purchasing was adding up to startling amounts of money. Simply going to the store to pick up miscellaneous items throughout the week or hanging out with friends frequently would total as much as a household expense. We knew that this area in our life had to be under control. If not, it would control us.

A joint account was opened in both of our names which functioned as our business account. This account would store all of our monies for the household. Every expense that was due for the month would be automatically drafted from this account. In addition to our joint account, we both had our individual accounts for savings and personal expenditures.

I believe more now than ever before that Derek and I share one common hobby: traveling. This is one of our favorite pastimes and quite frankly the most expensive one. In order for us to continue to enjoy the trips that we take, we had to take care of the house first and begin planning in advance. When Derek and I realized the spending power we had been abusing, we both made a plan to discuss our finances on a weekly basis. During "Pillow Talk," we laid out our individual expenses and developed a plan of attack. A list of our "expenses," as I've grown to call them, are written out.

PICTURE *Perfect*

Each month we would focus on a specific expense to eliminate. Through purposeful planning, we have created a path that is leading us to financial freedom. The relationship that I once had with money has been mended. I have a newfound respect for this tool and how to use it. We function as wealthy individuals by planning for the future and preparing beforehand. But if there is ever a problem in our finances, we know exactly how to deal with it.

Remember, our marriage was created by us. Each month the expenses for the house are covered by my direct deposit only. In other words, we run our business off of one income. We would then determine how much money was needed to cover the expenses like groceries, gas, entertainment, and unexpected situations. This calculated amount of money would be withdrawn from our joint account and placed in labeled envelopes. My debit card is taken out of my wallet for the month and remains unused. The only money that can be spent has to come from our envelopes. If we miscalculate for the month or simply deplete our funds, we cannot withdraw any money from our joint account or pull from any other envelope.

With Derek's income, he contributes a set amount to our savings account. It takes communication. It takes discipline. It takes practice. In the meantime, we are also strategically increasing money in our separate savings accounts. For example, I enjoy pampering myself. This money covers getting a manicure and pedicure and getting my hair shampooed and styled on a weekly basis. For Derek, it covers his nights shooting pool or watching the game with the boys.

This plan of action is working for now, but life changes. If we ever need to make adjustments, we have a strategy in place to do so. Our understanding of money has strengthened through active communication and our dedication to increase our empire. It's all about having and maintaining a healthy relationship with the Benjamins.

PICTURE *Perfect*

REFLECTION

1. What is your current relationship with money?

   _____
   _____
   _____
   _____
   _____
   _____

2. How important is money in your marriage?

   _____
   _____
   _____
   _____
   _____
   _____

3. List the expenses that you currently have and how this could possibly impact building your financial empire with your spouse.

   _____
   _____
   _____
   _____
   _____
   _____

DAY-TO-DAY *Operations*

Derek and I had to look at how we wanted our life to work as a married couple in business together. There were certain things that we had to have to make our lives functional. From the house that we live in, the appliances that we have, to our transportation, Derek and I had to determine what we needed in order to consider ourselves operative. When it came to the procedures of the house, we both had perceptions that the wife was always the homemaker, regardless if she had a job or not. That mentality wasn't going to survive in our modern-day living habits. I was a working woman, and he a working man. I felt that because we were sharing a partnership, that we both should be responsible for the upkeep of the house.

In our marriage, Derek plays the role of the CEO or head. He is the visionary and I help him to carry out the vision for our family. We opened our business daily around 6:30 in the morning. It was not just he and I, but also our infant daughter at the time. By Derek being a barber, he had an extremely flexible schedule. We discussed how our mornings of preparing for the day would play out.

PICTURE *Perfect*

While I dressed, he dressed the baby. As he dressed, I did her hair or fed her—depending on that day's agenda. Either I would pick up Demi from daycare, or he would. There was an understanding and constant communication. Furthermore, who would start dinner for the day all depended on who came home first. We both are capable of cooking, so he and I decided to share this responsibility. Speaking of eating, we both love to eat out. But this too was tallying a household expense. Derek and I agreed to dine out no more than four times a month. During the week, we focus on cooking and eating together as a family. We use this time to have open discussions about our day and to simply "check-in" with each other while breaking bread.

We had to know the expectations we had for each other. I knew that I was a clean person who kept the kitchen and bathrooms spotless. He, on the other hand, was used to dishes being stacked in the sink, clothes on the floor, and trash piling up. We had to come to an understanding of how our home would be maintained. It had to be orderly and somewhat consistent. I couldn't expect Derek to understand my way of thinking. I had been trained to upkeep a household; therefore, my natural abilities to clean were dominant traits. He didn't see the floor not being mopped or the bed not made up as a problem. We decided that we would share the chores of the house.

Since my parents' and friends' marriages played a significant role in establishing my views on marriage, I had to make sure that I was creating a new perception with my new husband and new life. The way we decided to run our business didn't have to look like anyone else's.

It just had to work for us.

The way the house functions also covers how we will train up our daughter, Demi. Notice that I didn't say raise her. When children are raised, they are brought up in a society that doesn't have the spirit of their parents. We made a conscious decision on how much television she would watch, which activities she should participate in, even the school that she would attend. Since Derek and I are Demi's first example of what a marriage looks like, we want her to see the love that we created in action—one day at a time.

PICTURE *Perfect*

REFLECTION

1. Seeing your marriage as a business, what are the things that you need in order to keep it functional?

   _____
   _____
   _____
   _____
   _____

2. Create a plan on how you see your marriage operating daily, weekly, monthly, and annually.

   _____
   _____
   _____
   _____
   _____

3. If you have or plan to have children, how will you and your husband train them to be significant figures in life?

   _____
   _____
   _____
   _____
   _____

IT'S OUR Anniversary

"A wedding anniversary is the celebration of love, trust, partnership, tolerance, and tenacity. The order varies for any given year."

– Paul Sweeney

I can't believe it's been one year already. The joy of announcing this status on my Facebook page wasn't the picture I expected, but the one I created. I would never say that being married is perfect, but it is most definitely a painted picture. The beauty in it all is that you are the artist. And I did it. I created the *Picture Perfect* marriage.

As I took the frozen cake topping out of the freezer, this ritual symbolized yet another accomplishment—we made it. Derek and I used to joke about going back to the drawing board just before we approached our anniversary. After evaluating the profit or loss incurred since the initial opening of business, we would see if any terms needed to be renegotiated before we proceeded with the original plan. Apparently the joke was on us because many areas that we thought were in place, had actually gone unnoticed. There were still some areas that needed improvement: Derek becoming less selfish, and I becoming more submissive. Good thing Derek

PICTURE *Perfect*

and I have a sense of humor most of the time. This allowed us to be extremely truthful with each other and open-minded to change. We exchanged our concerns through social intercourse and strategically planned a resolution to the area.

I found myself looking through my wedding album several times throughout my first year of marriage. It reminded me of how happy we were on "our day." It turned out that our destination wedding was a part of our story plot. Destination not only meant to travel for a wedding. For us, it meant that as a couple we were going somewhere in our journey as husband and wife. A traditional wedding wouldn't have captured what we were creating.

Just days before our anniversary, we hugged each other in the kitchen and began to relive the days when we were headed to Jamaica to get married. This time the year before, we were preparing to travel across the sea. I remember walking through the airport following Derek's lead as he carried a pink and black formal wear cover. If we were celebrities trying to be in disguise, we would've been attacked by adoring fans and paparazzi. People were shouting "Congratulations" as if we had "We're about to get married" lettered on the back of our shirts. We were excited. We loved the accomplishment we had made. We had invested the hours, studied our new roles and had gone through training. It was time for us to finally come together as Mr. and Mrs. What a feeling!

I placed the cake on the countertop. The cake that traveled across the beautiful Caribbean Sea, making it through customs, was about to be thawed. A soft grin graced my face as flashbacks resurfaced of us cutting into the bottom layer of the freshly baked cake. We were on the second floor of a closed patio at a resort in Jamaica. Our private dinner reception had just ended, and we were divvying out portions of cake to our guests. I remember the two-layered white cake with brown trimming centered on a small cake table draped in white linen. The cake was moist. It tasted delightful.

By the next day, the cake had finally thawed. I peeled back a corner of the crinkled aluminum foil as Derek looked on. Pieces of cake and icing were stuck to the top of the foil. But to our surprise, the cake was just like it was a year ago despite the color change of the icing. It was moist. I took a fork and placed a piece of the cake in Derek's mouth. He did the same to me. In an instant, we saw each other back to where we were.

Contrary to belief, my first year was not too much of an obstacle course; however, there were a few isolated challenges thrown in the pathway. That was expected. But it was the kind of bliss that I created. Again, the images of the fantasy world were our reality. The day that we exchanged vows had arrived. And on this day, love was truly created. The feeling that I had on this day symbolized all of the love that I knew would carry us through the first year and beyond.

Now, a year later, the same man who feared the unknown, had been won over into a reality that he didn't want to be without. Derek absolutely loves being married. Throughout the year I recall him just randomly saying how he was so glad that he married me. He demonstrated his words through the thoughtful actions he planned on our first anniversary. Real love filled my

PICTURE *Perfect*

heart as the man I married planned a memorable day that would demonstrate how much I meant to him as a wife.

Our anniversary made me feel perfect. Mini-cards in the color of our wedding theme were placed throughout the house. One positioned in front of my jewelry box in the bathroom. Another card was discovered resting on the box that protected a rich strawberry cheesecake with whipped cream. Each envelope had "10-10" printed on every corner. That was the day our lives began—together. There were five cards total. Throughout the day, Derek became the hopeless romantic that I always dreamed of. He was catering to me as if it were our first date. The words that he had written on the inside of the cards painted a picture of perfection. They shared the love that he had for me. He thanked me for being his wife. I must've been playing my position well.

After I married Derek, I felt powerful. I felt like I could do absolutely anything. There was excitement on the island. I felt adventurous. While in Jamaica, I felt a new freedom overtake my spirit. Maybe it was the act of letting go of what I once knew life to be and entering a new phase that I was in control of. As an act of my freedom I jumped off a twenty-five foot high cliff. I told you I felt like I could do anything. But it didn't stop there. The same feeling overtook me ironically almost a year later. To kick off my second anniversary weekend, I felt the urge to display my liberation once again. Now there is no ocean near the A-T-L, so cliff-diving wasn't an option. Plus it was autumn in the states. Not a good combination. Instead, I felt like I could fly. I went skydiving. It was the most liberating experience since I became Mrs. LB. My leap of faith just demonstrated how I felt at this point in my life: free. As a single woman, there was a lot of bondage there. But the shackles were released, and I was experiencing the picture perfect life.

My perception of love and being married had finally been confirmed. We really did love each other and had created the love that we believed would take us to the next level. I could finally admit that I had created a situation that I was in love with and would continue to play my role in order to keep it alive. Being married really isn't everything that the world makes it out to be, it's better!

When you really think about it, nothing is—until you customize it. A lot of life's most precious stages are fantasized. And the married life is no exception. The one thing that I do know is that I have the power from this day forth to continue to create my marriage into the Picture Perfect image that I want it to be.

Picture Perfect is not without flaws. It's full of flaws. I used to think that all of the bedtime story princesses lived a perfected life. But perfection is not being perfect. He's not perfect. I'm not perfect. But together we are **Picture Perfect.**

With almost two years under our belt and the plan to add even more to our status, what will be the blueprint? I know we've created the **Picture Perfect** one!

PICTURE *Perfect*

REFLECTION

1. How do you picture your first years of marriage to be?

2. What do you plan to do to make every day of being married an anniversary in itself?

3. Develop a plan of celebration for your anniversary. What will you do to recreate love on your special day?

REMEMBER WHY YOU SAID, "*I Do.*"

> Remembering when you said, "I Do" is easy.
> Remembering why, now that's special.
>
> – Lakia Brandenburg

I must admit. We were destined to be in Destin. To celebrate our sixth year wedding anniversary, we took a good ol' fashion road trip to Destin, Florida—home of the sugar sand beaches and turquoise water. The amazing weather (85 degrees daily), light, fresh breeze and complete relaxing atmosphere was exactly what we needed as a happily married couple celebrating our journey to making it last forever.

Just six years before, we were getting married and starting this partnership and now another chapter was being added to our version of our real-life love story. When your anniversary comes around, you can easily remember when you said, "I Do," but we often forget to remember why. As we reclined in our beach chairs under an oversized umbrella, all while listening to the waves crashing against the shore, we began to recall the moment that had brought us to another year as husband and wife.

How did we make it this far and still able to look at

PICTURE *Perfect*

each other with so much love and admiration? How did we manage to remain happy? With so many flaws, how are we able to see the good in each other? In all honesty, we're still imperfect. That hasn't changed. Derek still leaves the empty toilet paper roll in the bathroom, and I still unleash my Gemini twin from time-to time. But I must say that our relationship has greatly matured since we know what it takes to thrive as a couple and to continue to work for what we want in our marriage. With the continuous grow, the obstacles we're overcoming, and the intentions we're setting to stay happily married, it's all working together for our good. (This is *still* good work.)

Hubby and I both left Destin refreshed and with a new reason why we continue to say, "I Do." Here are five ways to make every anniversary special by not only remembering when, but *why* you spoke those two powerful words into existence.

1. Reminisce About Your Wedding Day
Anniversaries are the perfect time to think back to when it all began. Pull out your wedding book or search through old pictures and videos and relive the events from your special day. Think about how you felt when your wedding day finally arrived. If you wrote your own vows, reflect on the words you said and the meaning they may hold now. Read through any old wedding cards or well wishes that your guests gave to you. Take turns retelling your favorite moments and do your best to tap into the feelings you had on that day.

2. Define Your "Why" (Your "Why" Should Change)

When I stood under the gazebo in Negril, Jamaica to exchange vows, I knew why I was professing my love for Derek—I loved him and wanted to create a life with him. Now six years later, my "why" has become more detailed. The love I have for my husband is much deeper than it was before and you may recall that we were together almost ten years before we married. I didn't think I could learn anything else about him, and he didn't think he could discover anything new about me. But we did. We've grown more patient with each other and accepting of who we are as individuals. Our friendship has found new meaning and the appreciation we have for each other is more evident. Think about your why both then and now. Over the years, why you decided to become one should actually become clearer and be a testament of your growth as a couple.

3. Celebrate Your Love Story

Every wedding anniversary adds another chapter to the lives you are building together. Think about how you made it to where you are today (even if it were a struggle). What was the good, the bad, and the ugly of your marriage this year? How did this year add more value to your relationship and what lessons can you take with you into the next year? In what areas of your marriage do you need to improve (communication, finances, sex, etc.) Remember, you're creating your love story and learning to trust the journey that you're sharing together.

4. Start a Why I Said, "I Do" Journal

Every week or so, I post on social media (@TheWife-

Coach) the following statement: *"Remember Why You Said, 'I Do.'"* When communication becomes an issue and your marriage hits a bump in the road, that's when we want to question, "Now, why did I get married again?" LOL! Start a ritual where you stay connected to your spouse and marriage by writing down your emotions and matters of your heart. Ever so often, write down five reasons you're committed to your marriage and spouse and use this exercise whenever your marriage faces challenging seasons. Your emotions can add confusion and cause you not to think rationally. If ever in doubt, stay prayerful and optimistic and know that this season will pass.

5. Renew Your Vows

I don't know if witnessing two wedding ceremonies on the beach that day in Destin had me wanting to get married again or not, but who said that you need an actual ceremony to recommit yourself to your marriage? You can renew your vows without the wedding party or officiant present. And your anniversary is the perfect time. Remember, your marriage is your business. Take inventory of what's working and what's not working. What areas do you need to work on or invest in? Which areas in your life are you neglecting? Make a promise to each other to do better in the areas that need special attention: communication, trust, housework, sex, etc., then develop a plan to start making the necessary changes.

MEET LB

Lakia "LB" Brandenburg is fiercely committed to providing practical advice for women (who are married or planning-to-be) on how to live the happy wife life, and create and sustain a thriving, loving relationship with their husbands.

As an author, speaker, and wife coach, she is the trusted voice preparing women to become wives while educating and empowering them to know what to do, before and after they say, "I do." LB's "wives wisdom" and inspiration has been shared at conferences, on radio stations, television networks, and has been featured in magazines including *Rolling Out* and *Huffington Post*.

BE THE PERSON
you'd like to be
MARRIED TO

www.ingramcontent.com/pod-product-compliance
Lightning Source LLC
Chambersburg PA
CBHW052023290426
44112CB00014B/2353